For the Duration

Felicity in uniform, 1939.

For the Duration
A Lighthearted WAAF Memoir

Felicity Ashbee

Edited by Cleota Reed

SYRACUSE UNIVERSITY PRESS

∞ The paper used in this publication meets the minimum requirements of the American
National Standard for Information Sciences—Permanence of Paper for Printed Library
Materials, ANSI Z39.48-1992.

For a listing of books published and distributed by Syracuse University Press,
visit our Web site at SyracuseUniversityPress.syr.edu.

ISBN 978-0-8156-0971-1

Library of Congress Cataloging-in-Publication Data

Ashbee, Felicity.
   For the duration : a lighthearted WAAF memoir / Felicity Ashbee ; edited by
Cleota Reed. — 1st ed.
      p. cm.
   Includes bibliographical references.
   ISBN 978-0-8156-0971-1 (cloth : alk. paper) 1. Ashbee, Felicity. 2. Great Britain.
Women's Auxiliary Air Force—Biography. 3. World War, 1939–1945—Aerial operations,
British. 4. World War, 1939–1945—Women—Great Britain. 5. World War, 1939–1945—
Personal narratives, British. I. Reed, Cleota. II. Title.
   D786.A774 2012
   940.54´4941092—dc23
   [B]   2011049185

Manufactured in the United States of America

"War?" my American friends had said, "What war?"

"Hitler," I replied.

"There isn't going to be a war," they repeated complacently.

But I knew better.

—Felicity Ashbee

Dedicated to the memory of
Irene Swift Murphy (1918–2011)
Felicity's WWII pal

Felicity Ashbee was born in Gloucestershire in 1913 and was educated at various schools in Jerusalem and England. From 1932 to 1936, she studied at the Byam Shaw School of Art in London, and she later exhibited at the Royal Academy. During World War II, she served in the Women's Auxiliary Air Force, where she was responsible for some memorable amateur theatricals. After the war, she worked briefly with her sister Helen in Manchester designing textiles, and then settled in London. She was for many years a much-loved teacher of art at various girls' schools. Her first book with Syracuse University Press was *Janet Ashbee: Love, Marriage, and the Arts and Crafts Movement*, a biography of her mother. In 2008, on her ninety-fifth birthday, Felicity published the autobiographical *Child in Jerusalem*, a vivid account of the childhood she spent in the Holy City after the collapse of the Guild of Handicraft in Gloucestershire. Jane Felicity Ashbee, artist, designer, and writer, died on 26 July 2008.

Cleota Reed is an independent scholar who divides her time between London, England, and Syracuse, New York. She has published and lectured widely on aspects of the history of ceramic tiles and the Arts and Crafts Movement in America. Her books include *Henry Chapman Mercer and the Moravian Pottery and Tile Works* (1987); *Henry Keck Stained Glass Studio* (Syracuse University Press, 1983); and, with Stan Skoczen, *Syracuse China* (Syracuse University Press, 1998). The Arts and Crafts Society of Central New York has published her chapbooks about Felicity Ashbee, *Felicity as We Knew Her* (2011) and *Felicity Ashbee: A List of Her Literary Work* (2009). She is a scholar affiliate at the Department of Art and Music Histories of Syracuse University. She was for many years consultant curator of the Syracuse China Collections and Archives.

Contents

Illustrations

Introduction

FELICITY ASHBEE was born in Broad Campden, England, a village in the Cotswolds, on 22 February 1913. Her father was the prominent architect and designer Charles Robert Ashbee, a leading exponent of the Arts and Crafts movement. Felicity had many different talents and was active in many different realms, yet to everyone who knew her she was always the same person: direct, gregarious, young in spirit, open to the world, slightly eccentric, and deeply liberal. She never married, though she liked the company of men. By her own admission, she remained surprisingly naïve and innocent about many worldly matters. Active into her last years, Felicity died on 26 July 2008, at age ninety-five.

A somewhat briefer version of the preceding lines served to introduce an exhibition organized by Felicity's friends to celebrate her remarkable life. Held in April 2009 at the Court Barn Museum in Chipping Campden, Gloucestershire, and titled *A Life of Her Own,* the exhibition highlighted her life as an artist, designer, teacher, writer, and traveler. It brought attention to her political radicalism and her concern for social justice, as well as to her community leadership and many acts of charity. The exhibition also made it clear that Felicity had become the guardian of her family's memory, a responsibility that she took very seriously. She kept a remarkable archive of family papers, diaries, photographs, and memorabilia, including much about her own life.

Felicity was the second of C. R. Ashbee's four daughters (her sisters were Mary, Helen, and Prue), and the most widely traveled internationally. Even before she retired from the teaching of art at a private girls' school in London, she had traveled extensively on the Continent as well as in the United States, Russia, Turkey, and North Africa. In England and America she sometimes followed her father's footsteps as a speaker, telling his story in delightful slide lectures, often breaking into song as she recalled her early life in Chipping Campden. In these lectures, she modestly played down her own colorful career. But her years of retirement also brought forth book-length manuscripts. Two of these have already reached publication by Syracuse University Press. The first (2001) was her fascinating biography of her mother, *Janet Ashbee: Love, Marriage, and the Arts and Crafts Movement,* with an introduction by Alan Crawford. The second volume, *Child in Jerusalem,* is a memoir of her family's stay in the Holy City during the British Mandate, told in the third person by herself as a child. Victor Winstone provided an introduction. The first copy of this book was placed in her hands on the day of her ninety-fifth birthday, 22 February 2008. These two books were not her first publications. She had already translated texts from the Russian; she was fluent not only in Russian, but also in French, German, and Italian. She also published a number of articles and short stories.

A third book, *For the Duration,* deals with her experience in the Women's Auxiliary Air Force, and it is the most personal of her writings. It is a woman's story, an intimate, detailed, sometimes humorous account of her life in the armed forces during World War II. She relates how she and others coped with a war machine that desperately needed the help of women but whose male leadership did not quite know how to manage the sudden influx of females into its ranks. She ranges over the impact of war on families and individuals from all classes and walks of life, and she also observes much about people and places that transcends the urgencies of wartime.

Looming large in her account is the incredible monotony and boredom that overcame military personnel in remote outposts even while fulfilling important duties. She succeeded in bringing a much-needed spirit of vitality to the air force stations at which she served by organizing amateur theatricals. Her need to have a "show" in progress becomes a recurrent experience in her narrative.

In editing this account, I have done little beyond removing a good many exclamation points, elisions, and capitalizations that Felicity used for emphasis. As her friends remember, she spoke with very great clarity but also with markedly emphatic phrasings. As most readers will have no memory of her voice or manner, it has seemed best to reduce the number of these marks of emphasis when they are unnecessary for meaning. I have also clarified a few facts with notes.

Throughout her narrative Felicity presents conversations as she remembered them. She kept no war diaries aside from play scripts. While some artful reconstructions of dialogue surely played a part in the present memoir, those who knew her well will recall her remarkable memory for details of past conversations. The quoted passages in this book ought to be taken as faithful approximations—often very close indeed—of events recalled in minute detail. Although undated, the manuscript of *For the Duration* almost certainly dates from the 1980s.

I am grateful for the encouragement of Felicity's extended family of friends and relations, of which I feel so privileged to have been a part. Her nephews Richard and Francis Ames-Lewis graciously allowed me access to Felicity's manuscripts and offered help in many ways. I also owe special thanks to Alan Crawford, her father's biographer, who verified facts about her life; to Chris Lester, who contributed photos, pointed me to resources about the Chain Home radar system, and offered corrections to preserve the manuscript's "English English"; to Stephen Walton and Richard Slocombe of the Imperial War Museum for their help with the illustrations; to Heila Martin-Person of Legacy-Graphics who brought Felicity's old photos back to life; and to David Tatham, who read and reread the manuscript with me. The book is entirely Felicity's and if she were alive I am certain that she would add considerably to this list of acknowledgments. She would have especially expressed thanks to Irene Murphy, her last living WAAF friend, with whom in later years she met often to reminisce about the old days, even until the month she died. The photographs in the book come from Felicity's archives unless otherwise noted. Her wartime papers are now in the collections of the Imperial War Museum, London.

By chance, I have written this introductory note on the seventieth anniversary of Prime Minister Neville Chamberlain's declaration of war on Germany. Felicity often reminded her friends that she chose to enlist immediately after the broadcast of the declaration, and on 14 September 1939 she did. She remained a WAAF "for the duration."

Cleota Reed
3 September 2009

PART 1

The Best Kept Secret (In the Ranks)

September 1939–June 1941

1. Beginnings
1939–1940

"*WAR?*" my American friends had said, "What war?"

"Hitler," I replied.

"There isn't going to be a war," they repeated complacently.

But I knew better.

On a recent student holiday in Austria and Germany I had seen the Nazis in action. For a brief visit to a sister recently married to an American, I had just crossed over the Atlantic in a ship crowded with refugees. I was scared things might get going before I got back to Britain. But I made it.

Because I had good German, pretty fair French, and a little Russian, the Censorship Office seemed a suitable place to offer my services. Obviously no one else was likely to want me as I was, more or less, fresh from art school. So, no sooner back in England than I found out where the language exams were being held, chewed the end of my fountain pen over strange texts, and went back home again to Kent to kick my heels, impatiently awaiting a verdict.

But then came the traumatic moment on 3 September 1939 when our crackling wireless set gave Chamberlain's Declaration of War speech, followed by "God Save the King" and the Polish national anthem, which we heard for the first time. We, of course, stood to attention for both. Then, unbelievably, the first air-raid warning wailed into the September sky. My youngest sister [Prudence], with her three-week-old baby [Conrad] and German "Class C. Alien" husband [Walter Horst Nessler] had taken refuge with my parents, who in any case had had to "guarantee" him. He was a "political," and they had only managed to get him out of Germany just in time. Two rooms of the rambling Victorian family house had been made over to them. The baby in its pram was out in the garden, and there was a mad rush to trundle the precious newcomer to the supposed greater safety of the veranda. And then, nothing more happened.

But in the atmosphere of anticlimax in the days after this non-event, I grew unbearably restive. If Censorship didn't want me, I'd join up in the Air Force. I'd always wanted to fly! So a few days later[1] I found myself sitting in a makeshift recruiting centre, stuffy and smoke-wreathed, somewhere, I can't remember where, in London, signing on with the Women's Auxiliary Air Force (WAAF).[2] At least that ought to be within smell of an aircraft!

A dark-haired girl sat on the chair next me. It turned out that she was deserting her job as a continuity-girl at Ealing Film Studios and was also offering herself, full of patriotic fervour, to the cause.

My turn came. A glance at my curious non-credentials (who wanted anyone who'd had a picture "on the line" at the Academy?[3]) and I was labelled *Clerk*. The vision of Silver Wings receded and post office and bank grilles took their place.

"*Clerk!*" I exclaimed, chagrined.

"S/D," he added. "Special Duties." Obviously that was the only information we were to get for the time being. But the word "Special" was a slight amelioration.

---

1. Felicity enlisted on 14 September 1939, giving her full name, Jane Felicity Ashbee. Her service number was 885360.

2. In June 1939 King George VI established the Women's Auxiliary Air Force (WAAF) for duty in support of the Royal Air Force (RAF) during time of war. The WAAF was neither an independent military organization nor was it completely integrated within the RAF. Rather it served its "parent" force by substituting, wherever possible, women for RAF personnel. The WAAF was mobilized on 28 August 1939 and within the year tens of thousands of women had volunteered to serve. By 1945 a quarter of a million women had served in the WAAF in over 110 different roles, supporting operations around the world. They were an integral and vital part of the RAF's war effort. After the war the government formed, effective 1 February 1949, a permanent female peacetime force, the Women's Royal Air Force (WRAF), as an integral part of the RAF. See Beryl E. Escott's *The WAAF* for a concise and authoritative history of the women's Auxiliary Force in the Second World War (Oxford: Shire Books, 2007).

3. Felicity refers to the Summer Exhibition at the Royal Academy in London, where she had exhibited her painting *The Boaters* in 1937.

Soon we were summoned to report to Leighton Buzzard, to a large, shabby house whose neglected garden was knee high with uncut grass. In this garden, a somewhat morose Air Force Sergeant proceeded to try and instil into an embarrassingly motley un-uniformed bunch of women the peculiar rules of drilling and marching.

First came a mysterious business called Numbering Off in which we were eventually got into a line of approximate height. This in itself was quite a feat in all that long grass, with a lot of "Eyes *right*"-ing, and "Eyes *front*"-ing, which created a good many giggles, for there was no explanation as to what on earth it could all be *for!*

Then came an even more incomprehensible instruction. "For—orm *fours!*" yelled the Sergeant. Fours! But, *why?* And even more important, *how?* We milled around, bumping into each other and muttered phrases of "Hey! I was next to her!" and "But I'm taller than you!" There almost seemed to be elements of far-off childhood games where you dodged round moving bodies to try to get to a safer position.

The Sergeant's face went a shade more purple. We were, of course, sublimely unaware of the terrible indignity he was suffering. No solid line of male predictability at which he could swear in a normal barracks-room manner. No reassuring stamp of regulation boots to make him feel he was getting *any*where, just a shambling shuffle of often provocatively female forms dodging about to an accompaniment of increasingly hysterical giggles.

In the intervals of this curiously meaningless activity we were assembled into what must once have been an impressive drawing room to be given talks on the elements of Radar (so that was what Special Duties was going to be about, for those of us who had ever heard the word, that is) and a smattering of information, much of it as incomprehensible as it seemed irrelevant, from a fat volume called the *Manual of Air-force Law.*

On one afternoon we were sat down, offered sheets of paper, and asked to give a brief account of why we had volunteered to join the Service. My essay was short and passionate. I wanted to be part of something larger than myself, I wrote, and to do my small bit in the struggle against Hitler. I was, in fact, a child of my time, though I certainly did not describe myself thus. Nor did I offer any details as to my "political" past in my one page "testament" on joining up.

From the moment I had found John Reed's *Ten Days that Shook the World* (1919) in a Leftist bookshop I had been hooked.[4] With millions of others I had signed the famous Peace Pledge about not fighting in any circumstances for King and Country, and I had been shamed and unbearably moved by the plight of the groups of out-of-work, undernourished miners shuffling along the gutters of Oxford Street, singing marvellously.

But then had come the rise of Hitler, the re-occupation of the Ruhr, and the first evidence of the savagery of the Nazi regime. As a family we had a strong link with Germany because my paternal grandmother was from a Hamburg Jewish business family. Hamburg, of course, at the time she married my grandfather, did not consider itself to be German at all but was one of the proudly independent cities of the Hanseatic League.[5] But German was her mother tongue, though since her youthful marriage she had lived in England. My grandfather, dead, alas, long before my birth, had been an excellent linguist, and we still had links with the German cousins living in Hamburg, about whom anxiety grew as Nazi attacks on the Jews were stepped up. My sisters and I had all been sent after leaving school for periods of study in both Germany and France.

On my mother's side, my maternal grandmother had been born in St. Petersburg of a Scots family in the timber business, and thus spoke Russian and French as well as English virtually from birth. So my mother had also been bred in a tradition of multilingualism, and the idea that we should all spend some time abroad and be able to speak one or two foreign languages came naturally to us.

We happened to have a German boy staying with us as a paying guest during the summer of 1934. We hadn't realized how strongly Nazi his family's sympathies must have been until we saw his blanched face when

4. John Reed, an American journalist and socialist, witnessed the October 1917 Revolution in Russia. His account of the event, *Ten Days that Shook the World* (1919), remains widely known.

5. A fourteenth-century alliance of merchant associations within the cities of Northern Germany and the Baltics.

we told him of Roehm's execution for the alleged plot against Hitler. He packed his bag and left for home at once.

Only a month later came the attempted Nazi coup in Austria and the murder of Dollfuss in Vienna.[6] Yet both of these countries had been thought to be "civilized." By comparison, Mussolini's invasion of Abyssinia seemed less shocking, even though the Emperor Haile Selassie, the Lion of Judah, took refuge in Britain.

And then had come the Spanish Civil War [1936–39]. I was soon deeply involved. I designed banners for marches and posters for the committee for Spanish Relief. I was stunned by the horror of the bombing of Guernica [1937] and, as the plight of the Jews in Nazi Germany became more and more evident, I found myself increasingly on the side of those who felt Hitler must be stopped, at any price.

When Chamberlain came back from Munich with his "Piece of Paper," I could not face the mood of the crowds and instead sat through a terrible film called *The Sign of the Cross*, twice! It had Charles Laughton as Emperor Nero, fiddling while Rome burned, and Claudette Colbert as the Empress Poppaea, coyly and discreetly bathing in ass's milk. Elissa Landi played a Christian girl who I think was to be thrown to the lions. At intervals, there was a close-up of a sandaled foot grinding the sign of the cross into the dirt. When I finally came out, the streets were still full of jubilant people celebrating: "Peace in Our Time."

I have often wondered since what some of those other WAAF recruits gave as their reasons for joining up, though to me it seemed obvious. If, however, what I wrote ever got into the hands of the MI5 people with their obsession about "Reds under the bed," it may well have had something to do with what happened to me the following year. But I handed in my bit of paper with no qualms and got on with the next, less meaningful activity.[7]

6. The reformer Engelbert Dollfuss, then chancellor of Austria, was murdered by Hitler's henchmen in 1934.

7. Presumably, what she wrote never reached MI5.

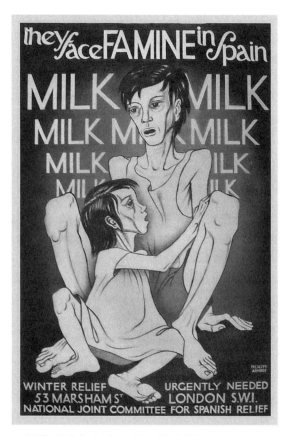

1. *Milk*, Felicity's Spanish Civil War poster, 1937.
Courtesy, Imperial War Museum, London.

There were as yet no uniforms; the only available items of equipment issued us apart from air-force blue raincoats and navy blue berets (goodness knows from where they had got such large quantities of them) were gas masks, and we were soon having practice runs on how to extract them quickly from their canvas covers, put them on, and breathe wheezily into them. They were of course intended exclusively for self-protection. His Majesty's Forces, even its female members, might find themselves in the vanguard of whatever was to come. But needless to say, they soon became the receptacles for everything a girl was used to carrying with her in her now forbidden handbag: powder compacts, lipstick and rouge, combs and mirrors nestled in the curled-up, vacuum-cleaner-like tube that brought filtered air into the face piece. As other items of uniforms began to appear, we were summoned to the makeshift Equipment Store to try them on and take possession.

Of course we had no inkling of why we had been recruited for these particular "duties." But behind the scenes it was already being realized that if Radar was to be fully effective, the educational and intelligence level of those working on it must be higher than that of the simple male "erks"[8] until now thought adequate for the job.

Erks were, after all, the product of the "3 Rs and Six of the Best"[9] type of education, which ended at fourteen and was totally lacking in any kind of science instruction or the suggestion that any language other than English might exist. At the time this was still all that was thought necessary for the working classes to be taught, or for those members of it who had not made it into grammar schools. No one who had got *that* far would have dreamt of joining up in any services in peacetime. The tradition for officers was different. There were families where sons followed fathers into the Army and the Navy via Sandhurst and Dartmouth. But not into the Other Ranks. Even in the worst depression years of the early to mid-1930s, the chronically unemployed did *not* rush to join any of the military services.

We Clerks S/D had at least *some* further education (i.e., we had stayed in some kind of school until sixteen or seventeen), though few if any of us had degrees or for that matter much in the way of maths or science training either. Such refinements were not thought essential for girls of any class; a little biology, or more likely only botany, albeit without much enthusiasm (I had dissected and drawn the odd buttercup). This was all that was offered on the science side in many girls' schools.

A large number of that first intake had been in boarding schools of the "gentlemen's daughters" kind (as I had attended for two hated and inglorious years), so to be back in the "dorm" at least presented no unaccustomed

8. Insignificant people; a general term of contempt, of military origin.

9. A beating by a teacher of six hits with a stick.

horrors to most of them. True, I was accused by my friend the continu-ity-girl, now ACW (Air Craft Woman) Pyddoke, soon known as Pyddy, of antisocial behaviour because I sat up in bed rustling my *New States-man* when everyone else wanted to go to sleep. I agreed she had a case but maintained that I had one also in wishing to keep myself adequately informed about the state of the world and the war.

Once our sketchy induction was behind us, we were posted to Head Quarters Fighter Command [HQFC], Stanmore, sorted out into either Fil-ter Room or Operations Room and then taken to our billets.[10]

It then soon transpired that, in the frantic rush at the outbreak of hostilities, the billeting officers had done their fact-finding at the double and had asked only how many "bodies" each of the small semidetached houses along Elstree Road could take, not how many beds were available to put the bodies into. This meant that I found myself, to the horror of my new and rather clued-up friends, sharing a double bed with a six-foot les-bian ballet photographer who, since her measurements were larger than anything the manufacturers of WAAF uniforms allowed for, continued for some time to wear her long black cloak and black sombrero, for all the world like the famous Sandeman Port advertisement. As it turned out I soon had the bed to myself, for she said sharing one with me was like sleeping with a dynamo. So she summoned a Lilo[11] from home and inflated it to fill the narrow space between the bed and the wall.

Actually, there were probably quite a number of lesbians (whether by inclination or necessity) among those first women to join up. It is hard in our outspoken world of today to remember the silence that surrounded such matters. There had continued to be a surplus of women in that gen-eration, and in a world where they were still expected to be primarily

---

10. In his *With Wings Like Eagles: A History of the Battle of Britain* (NY: Harper Collins, 2009), Michael Korda writes, "by 1939 most of the 'filterers' would be young women in the blue-gray uniform of the WAAF, who would soon be known, predictably, as the 'beauty chorus.'"

11. Air mattress.

wives and mothers, many who were going to have no opportunity of fill-ing those roles, jumped at the chance of joining one of the Services, and ultimately of wearing a masculine style of uniform as a way of persuad-ing themselves that they were not totally "surplus to requirements."

We soon discovered that HQFC itself was housed in Bentley Priory, a large, once-elegant mansion, originally set in 460 acres of woodland and meadow. In 1883, Edward Walford described it in his *Greater London* as "well sheltered by its own woods . . . and commanding most charming and panoramic views of its own beautiful terraces, gardens, lawns and undulating deer park, adorned with oaks, beeches and other grand forest trees."[12] Built in the 1760s, Bentley Priory had been largely remodelled in 1788 by the Marquis of Abercorn for his wife, Catherine, and their six children. Here in the sumptuous reception rooms which another chroni-cler, [Daniel] *Lysons,* described as "convenience united with magnificence in a manner rarely to be met with"[13] the first Marquis held the parties for which he and Bentley Priory became almost notorious. Amongst the many famous figures who frequented these "fashionable and intellectual gath-erings" were Sir William and Lady Hamilton (Admiral Nelson's Emma), Pitt the Younger, the Duke of Wellington, and the Prince Regent himself (later George IV). Sir Walter Scott is alleged to have sat in the seclusion of the little summer-house by the ornamental lake covered in water lilies, correcting the proofs of *Marmion.*

What glory remained of the mansion by 1939 was battered and scarred by adaptations, and the once beautifully landscaped garden was a wilderness overgrown and neglected through which, muffled in a strange assortment of garments, we stumbled in the blackout when coming on night duty during that first, bitter winter.

Many young people try to write poetry, and I was no exception. The verses that follow appeared in a short-lived *WAAF* magazine that Pyddy,

---

12. Edward Walford, *Greater London: A Narrative of Its History, Its People, and Its Places,* 2 vols. (Cassell, London: 1883–84).

13. Daniel and Samuel Lysons, *Counties of England,* 6 vols. (1806–22).

2. Bentley Priory in 2010. Photograph by Cleota Reed.

to fill in some of the off-duty hours, got permission to produce, and in which I collaborated. In fact, between us, we wrote the major part of three issues.

> A khaki coat lies on the marble seat,
> In the November rain the grass is sodden
> Muddied and brown. A hundred heavy feet
> On the deserted flower-beds have trodden.
> And still the cupids with their moss-grown urns
> Held high in stony hands, spill withered ferns.
> Into the misty sky the guns nose out
> From sand-bagged rings; sinister snouts of steel.
> The stone bowl where the fountain used to spout
> Is clogged with leaves. The stucco facings peel.
> But the cracked bell in the Italian tower
> Discordant, fairy-like, still tells the hour.
>
> Boots on the lawn, boots on the wide stone stair;
> Boots on the cellar flags, boots up above,

Blue cloth with wings, and gas-masks everywhere,
Where Nelson may have wandered with his love.
Did the bell warn them that their joy would pass?
And stranger-feet would trample on the grass?

I do not know which of the "noble suite of the reception rooms, all about twenty feet in height" that Walford described now housed the nerve centre of the Defence of Britain. Perhaps some still top secret file contains the requisitioning details? There had been a boudoir with "walls of embossed green silk, a lofty and spacious dining room, and a drawing room which measured fifty by thirty feet." Perhaps this was now the Filter Room with its map of the seas to Britain's east, from northern Scotland right round to Lands End? There was enough height in all of them to build the upper tier, a rough wooden and metal-scaffolded construction disfiguring what was left of the Adam-style detail and cornices and draped with cables and angled lights. On this upper level sat the Teller and the Senior Officers controlling proceedings, and from here, visiting Top Brass, when they came in, would look down on how the war was going

Perhaps the billiard room or the library now held the Operations Room next door, into which the Filter Room tellers fed their information? This Ops Room had a map of the whole of Britain, divided up into sectors showing the stations from which fighters would actually be sent up to intercept incoming enemy aircraft. It also showed the Observer Corps posts which confirmed with visual sightings what had already been "seen" far out over the sea on the radar screens, and which had been turned into a true track on the Filter Room table.

The twenty-four hours were split up into six watches of four hours each, and we Clerks S/D were also formed into watches A, B, C, and D. Shifts ran for a week at a time. Watch A, for instance, would come on from 0900 to 1300 and again 1700 to 2100. They would be taken over by Watch B who would be on duty from 1300 to 1700 and again from 2100 till 0100. (We soon discovered there was no "witching hour of midnight" in the RAF, and learned to call that previously romantic moment 23.59). And woe betide any WAAF Cinderella who was two minutes late! Watch C would then come on from 0100 until 0500, and Watch D from 0500 until 0900.

3. *Filter Room at Bentley Priory,* 1940. Drawn from memory by Felicity Ashbee.

Perhaps it was because of a time-honoured tradition that women should not do night shifts that those two watches were followed by a longer break than the day and evening ones. Even in the bad old textile mills of the north it had been recognized that women, who always composed a large part of the work force, would never get any proper rest if they worked nights because of family commitments. Of course, we were supposed to be spending the extra time off sleeping, but many of us didn't pay much attention to that and seized the extra hours to get away.

In the Filter Room, each position on the map was linked by land line to an out-station in some remote spot near the coast. Here a discreet hut or van held the small team manning the radar equipment with its television-type screen whose little green blips first hinted of a plane on the horizon. When something appeared on any of these out-station screens, the WAAF at the Filter Room end would be alerted and would put down a brightly coloured "tiddly wink" on the map table at the grid reference given her by her out-station opposite number. Each station had its own colour, and as there weren't enough colours to cover all the positions, care was taken that a colour was not repeated anywhere on the map where two stations could possibly be plotting the same aircraft. Thus the bright scarlet of Netherbutton in the Orkneys did not appear again until Stenigot in Lincolnshire, and then not again until Dover. These stations were unlikely ever to pick up the same response. The same applied with the other colours that had to be repeated. The tiddly winks had numbers 1 to 5 clearly marked on them, and had to coincide with the clock's minute hand, so no plot was ever more than five minutes old.

When one out-station's sighting was confirmed by another one picking up the same signal, the Filter Officer would "filter" or decide on the true track by putting one of his little arrows down on the trail of tiddly-winks. The Filter Officer's coloured arrows corresponded with the coloured segments of the clock, which changed every five minutes, thus enabling a check to be kept on the up-to-dateness of all the tracks. Once the "true" track was established by the Filter Officer, the grid reference of the point of the leading arrow would be "told" through to the Operations Room by one of the three Tellers sitting in commanding positions in the upper tier. The Ops Room WAAF with their long magnetic wands would then go into action on their own map. During the first months of what came to be known as "the Phoney War," we would often sit idle for the whole four hours!

Over the table's sulphurous expanse
The counters drop, the coloured arrows creep;
The drowsy Plotters sit in vacant trance,
Yawn as they plot, and potter till they sleep.

Till the stern-voiced Controller reprimands
Their laggard sense of duty, and at once

The knitting flickers through their fevered hands,
Two plain, two purl, three echoes, one response.
I cannot see what plots are at my feet,
Nor what fell strength the Nazi raid-plaques bear,
But still my voice, which once was low and sweet
Tells hoarsely thro' the unconditioned air.
Yet one thing cheers me, just to think of it,
Bored tho' I am to tears; perhaps there is
A Potsdam Filter Room where Brownshirts sit
With hands in lap, in boredom such as this![14]

But the authorities at least had the sense not to forbid us activities to keep us awake. So the WAAF positions would be encumbered with books, knitting, letter-writing materials, even chess sets. If my billet companion and I found ourselves on neighbouring stations she would produce her pocket set. She always beat me! Or I would bring my sketch-book and do quick sketches of Controllers, Filter Officers, or others. The habit of carrying it everywhere with me died hard, and no one objected. One of the last of these sketches, before the heat was really on in 1940, was of "Stuffy" Dowding himself, with his little-boy haircut and glumly brooding expression, almost as if he were remembering the Iron Duke's famous words about the only thing as sad as a defeat being a victory.

But there were of course the glorious twenty-four- or forty-eight-hour passes to break the monotony. On one of these I dashed all the way up to Morecambe Bay to see my older sister, Mary, whose husband Ted [Lewis's] department of the Charity Commission had been evacuated there from London. I arrived late on a dark winter's evening and found my way to their lodgings. Not daring to ring the bell so late, I used the time-honoured method of throwing gravel at the window, trusting to luck that it was the right one. It finally opened to show my sister's cautious head. There was always the risk of being accused by an Air Raid Warden of showing a

14. The Brownshirts referred to here were Nazi filter officers.

" stuffy" DOWDING   probably May 1940

4. Felicity's portrait sketch of Fighter Command's Air Chief Marshall Sir Hugh "Stuffy" Dowding. Pencil and ink wash on paper, May 1941.

chink of tell-tale light. I was let in and greeted with surprise and pleasure. Ted, though called up later into the Air Force, was then still a member of the Home Guard, not yet known as "Dad's Army" though it was always the butt of ribald jokes. The two of them were already tucked up in the brass-knobbed double bed, Ted's uniform on the chair beside it, his rifle propped dutifully nearby. We talked for hours and had a cosy night.

Or I would make a dash down to Kent to see how my parents were faring. The billeting officer's visit to them in the hectic August days had been just as cursory as the one in the Stanmore area. He had merely noted that the house had ten bedrooms, but not that this was an elderly couple. My mother [Janet] was sixty-two and my father [Charles Robert Ashbee] seventy-seven, with no resident help, in a place too large to manage but impossible to sell. Suddenly they were told to expect ten unaccompanied

5. Felicity on a visit to her parents in Godden Green, Kent. *Seated, from the left:* her father, C. R. Ashbee; Felicity; Mary Murphy (a London friend who came to help); and her mother, Janet, June 1940.

children between the ages of three and eleven! It never occurred to either of them to protest.[15]

True there was still a full-time gardener and his wife, who lived in a cottage that had been converted out of part of the old stables. Grace did come in and do the cleaning, and John did the boiler as well as keeping the family in vegetables. But as they had no children of their own they would not have contemplated tackling the task of looking after ten assorted and unknown brats!

So my mother simply sent an SOS to an old friend in London, a cleaning lady by trade, who responded at once, leaving her husband and three working sons to fend for themselves and bringing her afterthought eight-year-old girl with her. She set to without turning a hand to look after this extraordinary extended family, cooking for them, seeing all eleven

15. Children were evacuated to the country from London for safety from bombing.

through the Saturday night bath (a relic of the days when heating bath water in a "copper" was a laborious process, a deterrent to a daily bath), and checking them all weekly for head lice.[16]

My father even instituted reading aloud sessions with the older ones, who, with well-washed hands and de-nitted, smarmed-down hair, trooped into the library after tea for a daily instalment of *Huckleberry Finn.* The gang of assorted Cockneys walked daily, come rain, come shine, the couple of miles to and from the local village school at nearby Seal. When the first snows came, they had a wonderful time making snowmen and snow-balling in the spacious garden.

———•———

Those first months of the war were a strange, almost becalmed, existence at Fighter Command. But there was still quite a bit of time between shifts, so a girl on my watch named Fowler and I decided one snowy afternoon in January to take an exploratory walk across the fields. To our surprise we came across a ruined house about which there was something odd. Clearly it had not been destroyed by fire, nor by bombs, for the roof was intact. It looked as if it had been shelled. In a shattered ground floor room we found an inscription carefully pencilled onto a remaining area of plastered wall. It was dated Sept. 16th 1939, and read: THE WAR WILL END ON NOV: 27TH 1940. IT WILL GO ON IN FAVOUR OF GT. BRITAIN, FRANCE AND AMERICA. POLAND WILL BE RESTORED.

As bad luck would have it I hadn't got my camera with me, but I decided to come again the next day and photograph the inscription. It could be interesting. When I got there I first took several pictures of the outside of the house, then went inside. The inscription was gone! I felt a

16. Janet also engaged Mary Murphy to help care for Felicity's father, who was fatally ill with cancer. Mary arrived at Godden Green on 28 May 1940 and stayed for two years, until after CRA's death on 23 May 1942. In the diary Mary kept during WWII, her entry for 1 June 1940 reads, "It is lovely here. I can use the grand piano, have access to the library, can swim, take walks and listen to the enthusiastic talk of Felicity. She brought out a W.A.A.F. magazine which is very amusing, but it failed for lack of funds." Quoted with permission from Mary's son, Patrick Murphy. Mary made no mention of the children in the household.

frisson of unease but took myself in hand. What! A ghost house within half a mile of the Watford By-pass! Hardly!

When I got back the members of my watch greeted my tale with scepticism, even though Fowler backed me up.

"But I've taken pictures," I said.

"Oh yeah? What if they're all blank?"

But they weren't!

There was the house as large as life, looking like something out of World War I. I reckoned its date was probably turn of the century, so I managed to find a not *too* recent large-scale walking map to check it. But the place where the house by our reckoning was standing showed empty fields! It made a nice spooky story in our *WAAF* magazine. A pity though, that the end-date of the sooth-sayers proved to be so incorrect.

The Phoney War had other curious bonuses as well. My new friend Pyddy had been drafted into the Ops Room, whereas I was Filter. This meant we seldom went on duty at the same time, though when our time-off coincided we still hobnobbed together. She had just discovered she knew the wife of one of our more intimidating Senior HQFC Officers, Group Captain Turton-Jones.

Mrs. (Constance) Turton-Jones turned out to be the Susan Gillespie who had written a book called *The Man in Grey,* which had been made into a film on which Pyddy had worked at Ealing Studios. This gave her an opportunity of contacting Mrs. Turton-Jones on a basis that bridged gaps between ranks. For though it quickly proved impossible to enforce, female "Other Ranks" were not supposed to "frat" with Officers. What little hope there was of getting this across to some of the "society-oriented" Clerks S/D can be guessed from the two verses by Pyddy parodying the poet [John] Masefield, which we used in our *WAAF* magazine.

> Lovely, languid debutante going to the Grosvenor,
> Smug to the chaperones, seductive to the males;
> With diamonds for shoulder-straps, tiara and ear-rings,
> Blue lids, bare back, and bright red nails.

> Staid and simple WAAF coming out of the hostel,
> Enveloped in the uniform she couldn't well refuse;

6. "Lovely Languid Debutante." Felicity's drawing to illustrate the poem by ACW "Pyddy" Pyddock in the *WAAF* magazine, c. 1940. Ink on paper.

With grey stockings, gas-mask, beret and comforter,
Blue shirt, raincoat, and big black shoes.

But at least this connection meant that on occasions, discreetly, Pyddy and I would get the luxury of a civilized bath. This was followed by "silver-teapot-tea" in the very orthodox surroundings of the Group Captain's drawing room with its traditional floral chintzes on sofa and armchairs. This chance acquaintance was to stand me in good stead later, when I was "in disgrace."

And then, things really started happening in a big way. In April, the Nazis invaded Norway and Denmark. In May, Chamberlain resigned as Prime Minister and Churchill took over to make his "blood and toil" speech. The Maginot Line collapsed, Belgium capitulated, and the Germans swept into Amiens and Arras.

Chess sets, sketchbooks, magazines, knitting, and other impediments all vanished from the Filter Room. Suddenly, the war was for real.

2. The Phoney War Turns Real

1940–1941

BRITAIN WAS LUCKY to have had the breathing space of the "Phoney War" to get its act together before things really heated up. The vulnerability of Bentley Priory must have been a recurrent nightmare of the Defence chiefs during those bitter winter months of 1939–40 as work proceeded, literally digging "the Hole" in the Marquis of Abercorn's garden that was to become the new underground Filter and Operations (Ops) Rooms.

Meanwhile we WAAF were moved out of our billets into other more suitable accommodations. The Warren, another large, once beautiful country house not far from Bentley Priory, was taken over for some of the WAAF officers, and a number of the Ops Room watches. I had made friends with a corporal who had recently come to HQ Fighter Command from one of the outlying radar stations. Rita was lodged at the Warren, and I cycled up there to visit her. During that bitter, snowbound first winter of the war, the pond in the Warren's grounds froze over completely, and in no time at all the WAAF had dug out skating gear to make use of this rare opportunity while it lasted.

On a twenty-four-hour pass, when I had gone down home to see how my parents were surviving the "evacuee invasion," my mother, on hearing about our frozen pond and the WAAF exploits, said, "I believe Grandpapa's old skating boots are tucked away somewhere. They might fit you— he wasn't a very big man—if we could find them."

"Where on earth would they be?" I asked.

"Well, they might be in one of those old trunks that still have unsorted things in them, right up in the roof beyond the loft where the big boys are sleeping," she said.

The big boys were the older evacuees. Lennie, the most senior (though one of the most nit-prone!), was rising twelve, so he slept with two or three of the next in age, farthest away from our "house mother," Mrs. Orford. These boys were less likely to need any comfort during the night.

It was Lennie's dark-haired, six-year-old brother Ronnie who became an inseparable buddy of another six-year-old, the lint-headed Peter. They had been seen early on in their country life experience standing together looking speculatively at the cows in the field, so deceptively close, just the other side of the "ha—ha."[1] After long inspection, Ronnie was heard to say to Peter, "Pete! Cows what 'as titties for milk ain't got no place to weedle from, 'as they?" The blond and the dark heads were close together as they debated this knotty problem. Luckily one of the cows soon did the necessary, thus solving the anatomical equation.

The children all slept up in the attics, beyond the little bridge with its Victorian, church-style Gothic balustrade. These had originally been the servants' quarters in the days before my father had restyled the house for slightly easier, servantless, 1930s living. They were really just attics now anyway, not much more than raftered roof-space where an area had been cleared for the camp beds of two or three of the older children.

And lo and behold. When I got up there and looked, there in one of the battered, well-travelled, leather-covered and cotton-lined Victorian trunks, were my Scots grandfather's boots, with skates firmly screwed on, well greased and wrapped in old newspaper. And they fitted me. I bore them off in triumph and had a lot of fun trying to learn to skate before the weather changed. Rita must have acquired some skates from somewhere too, and we circled the pond, propping each other up to keep our balance.

For those of us not housed at the Warren, much less salubrious quarters were requisitioned down along the Elstree Road. These were a strange group of battered, maroon-painted, corrugated iron huts, whose origins were hard to guess at. Small partitioned-off rooms, not much larger than horse boxes, ran along one side of a corridor. Each of these now slept three or four WAAF, whose narrow little regulation iron bedsteads were separated from one another by orange-boxes, if you were lucky enough to find a greengrocer who still had one from the glorious days before the Nazi

---

1. A walled ditch or "sunken fence" serving to contain grazing animals.

submarines started interfering with supplies of "Jaffas" from Mandate Palestine. In one week alone in November 1939, 60,000 tons of shipping was sunk off the east coast of Britain as a result of the magnetic mines laid by the U-boats. Not surprisingly, we weren't told those figures; we just noticed there weren't any more oranges.

When stood on end, these boxes, which were about fifteen inches square and two feet-six inches in height, with a subdivision in the middle, were sanctioned by the authorities as lockers. So long as a bit of material was tacked over the front, concealing the regrettably feminine personal belongings stuffed within, a blind eye was turned.

One of the four girls squashed into our small "horse-box" was, I later learned, a Catholic. Being totally uninterested in religion or religious denominations, it was not something that I would have bothered about anyway. But later, I wondered if it could have been a factor in what soon happened.

On 30 November 1939, the Russians invaded Finland. As long as a month before then, the writer Laurence Housman, a great friend of my parents, had written to my mother saying he could not but be sardonically amused by Russia's behaviour.

> Here has our government for years been in such deadly fear of Communism catching hold in Italy, Germany, and Spain that it was truckled to dictatorship and helped to weigh the scales against all Left-wing movements, meanwhile severely snubbing Russia and running down all Russia's feelers for disarmament and peace conferences. And then, faced by Chamberlain's blundering policy to try and shape a hasty peace front with Russia, and failing . . . but having so frightened Hitler in the attempt, that Hitler was driven to make an agreement with the object of his detestation. . . . Then, to prevent Hitler from getting the whole of Poland, Russia has to unite in aggressive benevolence. . . .
>
> And behind all this manoeuvring and countermanoeuvring, Poland's thoroughly bad record ever since the Great War [1914–18], when she insisted on having more of the mixed population of East Poland–White Russians, Ukrainians, and Jews—to be under her rule than the great Powers thought she had any right to; and on top of that made

aggressive war against Russia to get another bite! Now Russia is simply taking her own back again, with a bit more! And though we did not denounce Poland for her aggression on Soviet Russia, lots of people have nothing but bad words for Russia in this countermove.[2]

Looking at the map it was not really surprising that, in spite of the August 1939 Non-Aggression Pact between Germany and the USSR, the latter should now be trying to make buffer areas—Finland and the three Baltic States, Lithuania, Estonia and Latvia—between herself and what had until then been a sworn enemy. The memory of the attacks on the young and emerging Soviet Union in the early 1920s, from all her Western neighbours, was still green, and the frontier between her and them was long and vulnerable. But the British reacted sharply and emotionally to the Finns' call for help, though what was offered did not in the end alter the course of events. By March the Finns and the Russians had signed a peace treaty in the Russians' favour. I can dimly remember my Catholic roommate's shock that anyone could ever say anything *not* attacking a Russian action.

On the other side of the corridor was the Rest Room with a few disintegrating, club-style chairs. I think there was also, somewhere, a Ping-Pong table. The more professional name of table tennis was not in current use then. In fact there were endless jokes about how such items of sporting equipment had to be listed in RAF inventories where the word order was, by regulation, reversed, i.e., "Item: Balls, pong, ping, airmen, for the use of." Seeing that here, in legal parlance, as the sex was not specified, the "male would embrace the female."

Leading out of the Rest Room was the "Mess," as we had now got used to calling the dining room. For those of us without military backgrounds, the vast majority, the name seemed curiously appropriate to the food we queued up for.

Some time in March, one of the Filter Room watches, mine as it turned out, was moved out of the huts to take up residence in the attics of a

2. The letter is now housed with the Ashbee papers at King's College, Cambridge.

convent a few hundred yards further along the Elstree Road. In the lower floors of this huge, castellated Victorian edifice the nuns in their sombre black-and-white habits continued in their withdrawn world while we carried on (perhaps in more senses than one) in the attic floor above them.

That does not mean that there was any wild living it up. There was no contraceptive pill then, and the fear of pregnancy kept a lot of girls on the "straight and narrow." A great many of them too had been brought up to believe you should wait for "Mr. Right," though how you were expected to know if that was what he was when he got all amorous and promised the world, no one ever quite explained. It was often the nicest girls who got "caught" because they couldn't believe their current admirers weren't telling them the truth.

But we did have the odd, discreet party up there above the nuns—girls only, of course—and it was at one of these that I had my baptism of fire regarding drink. As a family we had not been pub-frequenters. It was not my father's style of drinking, and we were four girls without brothers. So though it was not a case of anyone having "signed the pledge," there had been no drink in our home, apart from cider. My father had been at university with Fred Bulmer, who went on to make the Bulmer's Woodpecker Cider empire. Indeed it was always hoped that one of the Bulmer boys would possibly marry one of the Ashbee girls, but such parental wishes are seldom fulfilled. To my mother, cider seemed sufficient stimulus (and expense) for ordinary social intercourse, and my father didn't give it a great deal of thought anyway.

Having myself been a somewhat late developer regarding boyfriends, I had not had much opportunity to learn any drinking rules. I didn't realise that my watch had decided to rectify this. "What'll it be, Ash?" asked the ringleader, one of the tall, blonde, jolly-hockey-stick types, very casual-like, "Gin and lime?" It sounded safe, even familiar. I said, "Fine," and was handed a heavy glass tooth-mug apparently full of water. I had no idea what a tumblerful of gin with a dash of lime, as in fact it was, should taste like and proceeded to drink it as though it were lemonade. It crossed my mind that everyone was grouped rather closely round me, all apparently hanging on my words in an exceedingly friendly way. But I went on chatting. When I felt I'd done my stuff for long enough (the room did seem to be getting peculiarly hot), I said, "Well, that was a nice party, thanks a lot. Oh, and to show you I'm not drunk, would someone like to draw a chalk line to the door, and you can watch me walk along it as I leave?" I proved my point! And of course no one knew how terribly sick I was when, just in time, I reached the safety of a toilet. I have never very much cared for the taste of gin, or lime, since then. But my shares went up with the members of my watch!

Our navy berets had by this time been replaced by proper caps with shiny black peaks, and we were instructed in how to keep our cap badges, as well as our buttons, shining. Other more intimate items of clothing had appeared too, though many of our Clerks S/D looked with disbelief at the four pairs of "issue" woollen knickers (the word "panties" was unknown then) with elastic at waist and knee. Two were navy blue, and two a pale-ish air-force blue, which washing rapidly turned into a tasteful heliotrope, nicknamed at once, inevitably, "black-outs" and "dim-outs." Many of the girls carried on defiantly wearing their prewar, so-called, "French" knickers, but there were no actual body searches to see if the issue ones were in use.

Regarding bras, there were offered none at all to begin with, such things being beyond the imagination of peace-time Equipment Officers. In fact a joke on the subject was soon going the rounds. Two RAF officers are propping up a bar. The senior—in both senses of the word—says to the junior, "Brassiere? Isn't that one of these new fangled places where you can get a drink?"

"Brasserie, Sir? Well . . . not *that* kind of a drink, Sir."

But when it came to Kit Inspections, the great thing was to have the full complement of garments, or a credible laundry list to vouch for the missing items. Many of the places where WAAF were living, whether billets or Nissen huts, had practically no washing facilities, so a free laundry service had to be organized to which they could send their dirty washing. There was something else too that the regular Air Force, when catering for its female counterpart, had overlooked, not altogether surprisingly. This was sanitary towels.

I don't remember just when it began to be realised that WAAF would often be stationed in places miles from ordinary chemist shops where such necessities could be got hold of. Eventually it was the Lord Nuffield, one time plain Mr. William Richard Morris and currently, amongst many other activities, chairman of Morris Motors Ltd., who came to the rescue. Who put him up to it, I don't know, perhaps his wife, but as most historians have tended to be male, such embarrassingly female—though vital—details have often gone unrecorded. (Were they manufactured in a secret wing of the factory as a by-product of the Morris Minor?)

All we knew was that these essentials arrived at Equipment Stores sewn into huge sacking rectangles, probably 50 or 100 packets at a time, and were then issued one packet per WAAF per month. The only trouble was, they were found to be essential for many other purposes too. They turned out to be wonderful for all kinds of polishing as well as serving a useful purpose for WAAF struggling to sleep after night duty. A "Nuffield ST" looped round a door handle was a great help against banging doors.

Needless to say, a variety of wiles were resorted to in order to acquire additional supplies. We had quickly learned how to stack our "biscuits," the three square bits of mattress that fitted the iron bedsteads and had to be piled on top of each other with the folded blankets and sheets on top again. The sheets, we were told, were a concession to the "gentler sex." Erks had to sleep in the rough brown issue blankets, and like it! We soon reduced this bed-making process, time-wise, to a fine art, as it always had to be done on getting up, at whatever hour.

Our new subterranean work place, The Hole, was ready just in time for the end of the Phoney War. The official records say that the change-over, which meant the entire linking up of the Radar system of the outstations with HQ Fighter Command, "was completed in the short space of two and a half *minutes!*" Relief at Air Ministry must have been more than audible. We merely knew that instead of entering by Regency portal and marble staircases, we now squelched over duckboards covering seas of mud as we went truly underground to our new and much more purpose-built accommodation. True, the woodwork was in places rough and unfinished and calculated to ladder even the tough grey lisle stockings which now encased our legs. Trousers came in only quite a bit later for the likes of us. MT Drivers, Fitters, and Balloon crews were amongst the first to be allowed to wear them.

The new premises were at least functional. Some despised planner had even got around to making sure there were good angles of vision, especially for the three Tellers, who, once the big raids started, needed every help to cover the mass of multicoloured tracks between the dodging heads of plotters bending over to put down their counters and of Filter Officers filtering the true tracks of incoming enemy aircraft.

And then, as Hitler's armies swept into the Netherlands, Belgium capitulated, and the "Little Ships" began the unbelievable rescue of the waiting thousands from the Dunkirk beaches, disaster struck me personally in a totally unexpected way. The words "Quisling" and "Fifth Columnist" had by this time entered the English language, and certain government departments obviously panicked at the thought of how many of these hidden enemies might have slipped into the country in the guise of Jews or "politicals" escaping Nazi persecution.

My German brother-in-law [Horst] was still living peaceably with his wife and child [Prue and Conrad] at my parents' home in Kent. As an alien he was in any case not eligible for any kind of war service. Now, at breakfast time on a summer Sunday morning, two plain-clothes men appeared, and he vanished without warning or explanation in one of *our* police vans. It was only after six weeks of hard work on my mother's part, using every contact she had, that she learned that he was in Huyton Internment Camp near Liverpool. It was from this camp that the ill-fated *Arandora Star* collected her complement of volunteer internees to transport them to Canada for safer incarceration. Among the many genuine refugees who had been rounded up in that May swoop, there were, of course, some Quislings who volunteered to go to Canada in hopes of a better chance of escape over the unmanned frontier into the anonymity of the neighbouring United States. With this in mind, a number of them asked internees who preferred staying behind barbed wire in Britain if they would change names with them. For whatever reason, some agreed to do this.

When the *Arandora Star* was torpedoed, there was confusion as to who had gone down with it. The internees at Huyton who had exchanged names hurriedly came forward to explain that they were still alive. Horst had prudently steered clear of any such entanglement. When the chance came a few months later to volunteer for the noncombatant Pioneer Corps, he offered his services. He was released from the camp to chop trees in the Forest of Dean, where his family was able to rejoin him.

It was almost at the moment of his disappearance that I was suddenly removed from the Filter Room and told I could no longer work on Special Duties. Instead, I was to remain with my watch pro-tem and was relegated to brewing cups of tea and handing out bits of cake in the underground canteen which served both Ops and Filter Rooms.

Why? Any queries on my part were met by either stony or embarrassed silence. Some members of my watch even seemed to be treating me warily. Whatever had they been told, or what were they imagining? Was it Nazis the authorities were afraid of? Much more likely, Reds! Either way, whether the intention of those who had issued the order was to frustrate a Quisling (or a female Apostle[3] in the making?), it didn't seem to have occurred to anyone that I would be in a much better position to collect and disseminate information inconspicuously. This would be in the fetid intimacy of the canteen, rather than when actually hard at work telling in the Filter Room. That was beyond MI5's (or whoever else's) thinking.

It was even hinted that no one would object to my taking discharge from the service altogether. This was quite easy for WAAF in the early days. Later you had to prove you were married, and later still pregnant, before you could apply for discharge. My friend Pyddy had in fact already left, feeling her talents would be better employed elsewhere than by waving her magnetic wand over an empty Ops Room table. She spent the rest of her war in the Ministry of Information.

But I turned stubborn. I was indignant, mortified, and rather scared, but I was not going to go without a fight. But to whom could I turn for advice? I suddenly thought of Group Captain Turton-Jones, though not without some hesitation, because I sensed that my "Red" past, though it had never actually come up in Pyddy's and my social contacts with him, would be anathema to his orthodox view of things. He was, after all, a Regular. But I took a chance and approached him. He must have believed

---

3. Ashbee probably means a Judas-like traitor.

me, and I think he liked me—or found me intriguing—and his sense of justice was of the Voltaire brand. Even if my views were to him outrageous or incomprehensible, I had *Rights* and he told me what they were, and exactly what I could and should do about them. "Fill out an application form to see the Station Commander," he said. "If he refuses, you can go over his head to higher authority, King's Regulations."The Flight Sergeant from whom I had to get the form knew all about me and tried to put me off. "Come along now, Ash, what do you want to see the CO for? E's a busy man. Much better just go quietly."

"What do you mean, go quietly?" I asked belligerently. "What have I done wrong? Is it because I've been to Moscow?" I asked, attack being the best form of defence, they always said. "What about having been brought up in the Holy City of Jerusalem?" But that was too difficult for him. He handed me the form, and I filled it in.

It came back a fortnight later with a small message handscrawled across the top corner. "No good purpose is to be served by seeing this Airwoman at present." Right, I thought. Next step, my Chief WAAF Officer. I applied to see her, and entered saluting smartly. She had obviously been briefed. "What's all this about Communism, Ashbee?" she asked in her knife-edged Scots voice.

"I don't know what you mean, Ma'am," I counterattacked. "Is it because I have a refugee German brother-in-law? You are perhaps unaware that Corporal Pemberton is still working in the Ops Room? She spent her childhood in Germany in the Hitler Jugend."

In the pause while she considered these two unexpected statements I slipped in, "The Station Commander's refused to see me, Ma'am. I wish to apply to Higher Authority."

"You can't do that, Ashbee," came the acid response.

"Excuse me, Ma'am, but I understand that I can."

"How do you know?"

"King's Regulations, Ma'am!"

"Who told you?" the voice was even more edged.

I hesitated, then plunged, "Group Captain Turton-Jones."

There was a half-swallowed grunt. "Well, he's a Regular," she conceded reluctantly, "He ought to know. Fill in a form."

Eventually, I saw the WAAF No. 2, Trefusis-Forbes's deputy, who heard my story sympathetically enough and said she would "see what she could do." She must have done something, for a month or so later I was summoned to see the head of the RAF Special Police.

"Ashbee?" he said as I saluted, "Take off your cap and sit down." I was surprised. This was always a sign that rank was temporarily set aside in favour of a heart to heart.

"Cigarette?"

"Oh . . . thank you Sir!"

"I thought perhaps you'd like to hear some of the Police reports about you."

"Oh! . . . Very much, Sir," I said, genuinely intrigued.

"Here's one, typical of several," he went on, pulling out a paper from the pile in front of him. "Nothing of an incriminating nature having yet been said by this Airwoman, we advise a further period of waiting and . . . watching . . ."

"Watching, Sir? Watching . . . er . . . what?" I asked.

"Well . . . er . . . Ashbee, it's all this . . . er . . . stuff about . . . er, Communism."

"But, Sir," I said innocently, "I thought we were fighting Hitler, not the Soviet Union!"

He put a finger in his collar as though it were suddenly tight. "Well . . . er, it's a little more complicated than you might think . . . er, Ashbee," he murmured. He knew, and I knew that he knew, that "those above" had only been trained to look for Reds-under-the-bed. Fascists had always seemed a much more OK thing than those terrible Bolshies. After all, Mussolini had made the Italian trains run on time, hadn't he? And the idea that you couldn't take "that awful little man with the Charlie Chaplin moustache" *seriously* died hard.

"Anyway, Ashbee, here's the final report," he said. "This department having come to the conclusion that this lady (I controlled my features with difficulty, I liked that! Not Airwoman this time, but *lady!*) need no longer be considered as *dangerous,* we hereby recommend that she be reinstated in her previous employment, etc., etc."

"So you're in the clear!" he finished, looking up at me with a suppressed flicker of a smile. "Just be a trifle more . . . er."

"I'll try, Sir, and thank you!" And putting on my cap again, I saluted, did a flash regulation turn, and marched out. We had quite a reinstatement party!

I was on duty again with my old watch the next night, my telling skill unimpaired by the many weeks spent picking sodden cigarette ends out of tea-sloshed saucers in the steamy, gossip-filled, underground canteen. My Corporal's tapes, delayed by my period of disgrace, soon caught up with me too, and I sat down on the edge of my bed and sewed them on with care.

3. Raids and Recreation

1941

BY AUGUST the Battle of Britain, as it came to be called, was at its peak. I remember thinking how silly it was to label it that way, as if it were a single battle, like Agincourt or Waterloo, whereas in fact it went on day after day, with alerts and sirens wailing and dog-fights overhead, for what seemed like the whole summer. Nevertheless, one day in mid-August 1940, 180 German planes were shot down, and before that month was out came the first real all-night raid on London. From then on we would often come up from the Hole after an evening or night shift to see the white fingers of the searchlights crisscrossing the blacked-out dark, then suddenly pick up, and hold a tiny, mothlike plane. Or we would stare, shocked and disbelieving, at what should have been the pearly grey of the first light and see instead, the sky dawn red. It was not the dawn, but the red from the flames of burning London.

> And once again the moon is round and full,
> The May sky clear, almost too light for stars
> A lovely night to kill by . . . or to love,
> Were moons still made for lovers. But instead
> They point the raider where to drop its load
> And smile. And the proverbial nightingale,
> Shell-shocked to silence cannot lift her head.
> Her brown breast pierced by shrapnel, not by thorn.
> And we like moles, come up from underground,
> And over London see the flush of flame,
> And the slow cauliflower of purple smoke;
> And the May night seems colder as we watch
> The beauty and the horror and the waste.

And when at last through the thick pall of dust
On twisted girder and on smouldering brick
The morning breaks—perhaps another Christ
Weeps in the ruined streets of Bermondsey.

As we came off duty from those 1 a.m. to 5 a.m. shifts, we were usually able to guess what the chances of travel were likely to be from the pattern of raids we had left on the map when the next watch took over. Sometimes we hardly got anywhere before we had to start coming back again, but we were young, and sleep didn't seem as important as lots of other things. Even so, a snatched half-day was only worth it when we were on the shift that came off at 5 a.m. and we could catch the first Underground from Stanmore, if it was running. We would come up in Trafalgar Square, to trample through shattered glass and tangled fire hoses to see if there were any trains from Charing Cross for a dash down home.

Surprisingly, there often were! If not, we would hitch. Sometimes I would have a friend with me; Rita quite often came if our times-off coincided, and if so, we went home for twenty-four or forty-eight hours. We would be bearing the prized, unexpired portion of the day's rations, an ounce of tea and sugar in a careful screw of paper—no plastic bags then— or a rasher of bacon, even a snip of ration card which could be saved until the advent of "points," or a rare, tiny tin of salmon or golden syrup (bacon, butter, and sugar had come out on ration in January 1940).

But that spring both my parents landed up in hospital, having succumbed to the strain. The evacuee children had been moved elsewhere. In any case, once the raids really started, that part of Kent soon became known as Hell-fire Corner and hardly a place of refuge.

When my parents were recovered enough to come back home, a quieter regime had to be instituted, for my father, though probably never really aware of it himself, had been found to be suffering from inoperable cancer of the prostate gland. Since my mother increasingly needed moral and physical support to cope, a friend of a friend, Mary Murphy, herself in need of a home, came to be an extra pair of hands.

The gardener John's wife, Grace, did the cleaning, and another neighbour's wife from one of the nearby cottages helped with the cooking. John just managed to prevent the huge garden from going totally back to nature and kept the family in vegetables with probably compulsory surplus for disposal. Unless he suffered from some ailment of which I was unaware, this may have been tantamount to a "reserved profession," so that he did not have to be called up.

I still came down as often as I could manage it, with or without a friend, and my father loved hearing our accounts of the people who had given us lifts. One such hitch with a lorry to friends in the West Country specially delighted him. As we were crossing Runnymede, the chatty lorry driver remarked: "And 'ere's Runnymede, where li'l old King John signed the Magna Charter [sic] a few years ago, with all the Union men standin' lookin' on to see 'e done it proper. We'll 'ave ol' 'Itler 'ere signin' things some day . . . if 'e's lucky!"

Meanwhile the war spread. Immediately after Dunkirk, Italy came in on Germany's side. In July Britain sank the French fleet in its North African harbours, and the Vichy Government broke off relations with Britain. Abyssinia, British Somaliland, Greece, and Crete all became involved in the conflict. The number of National anthems of overrun countries, which in the first months had prefaced the evening news bulletins, had become so numerous that they had to be cut, first to an opening bar (people, however patriotic, could not stand to attention in their sitting rooms or work places for too long); then they were abandoned altogether.

More and more U-boats filled the Atlantic. The night raids intensified, and London's deeper Underground stations became the accepted harbourage for hundreds of families. The children would come "home" from school, unroll the family bedding (well behind the thick white line painted on the platforms to give free access to the train users), and, oblivious of the noise and the crowds of passengers, settle down with their comics to await their parents return from work. A kind of cheerful community spirit could almost be felt as you went down. The smell was a mix of monkey-house and urinal, for there was no way of air-conditioning these improvised shelters. There were "Elsans"[1] screened by sacking at the ends of most platforms.

---

1. Brand name of a chemical toilet.

We were never given exact figures of where the raids had been or what the casualties were, though it is now public knowledge that in 1940, in November alone, the toll of deaths in air raids over Britain totalled more than 4,500.

"Blitz" joined "Quisling" as a household word, and "Lord Haw-Haw" was constantly quoted.[2] The strange thing was, though, that you hardly ever met anyone who had actually *heard* him. It was always someone else who had told someone else, of what he had said. But soon another phrase appeared to buoy up flagging spirits. It was: "for the duration." Nothing could last forever. Most things were endurable if they were only for the duration, even massacres, which in London came to be almost routine.

In November 1940, we had a direct hit on the convent. We were not due to go on night watch for an hour or so, but the sirens had gone long since. Except for the drone of bombers we had almost forgotten there was a raid on. Sometimes we would hear a whole stick of bombs fall, then the second, apparently almost upon us, and I heard a voice which I only afterwards realized had been my own shouting, unbelievably: "On your stomachs, *pals!*" Surely *not* my vocabulary. But it worked!

Everyone threw themselves on their faces; the third bomb struck with a force that made our attic feel we were on top of an upturned pendulum sweeping us backwards and forwards across the surface of the floor. One girl panicked, but I was able to grab her hands and hold her reassuringly. Another, who fortunately for her was wearing her usual earplugs, sat up in bed with a shout and a second's delayed action because of them, just after the windowful of glass had shot like a cloud of arrow-heads across the room over her still prone form.

The last of the sticks fell beyond us as the plane receded. We discovered we were all more or less undamaged. I collected my flock, and we went down to report: "all present and correct," to find the central section of the convent a heap of rubble and some of the nuns down in the cellars

2. Lord Haw-Haw was the name of announcers on English-language propaganda radio programs coming from Germany, notably William Joyce, Britain's notorious traitor, who was executed after the war.

injured, though none were killed. I even sneaked out the next morning and took some illicit photographs, which I still have.

In May 1941, a single land mine was dropped in Chelsea, destroying several of the houses designed by my father on Cheyne Walk. It was a great blow to him because No. 74 was the house he had built as his and my mother's first home after their marriage in 1898. They had lived there for only four years before he had moved his idealistic Guild of Handicraft from the East End of London out to the Cotswolds. Now, in 1941, he wanted to see what was left, perhaps in a sense to say good-bye to the little Chelsea house that represented a special moment in his life. So, as he was no longer fit enough to make the journey by train—you never knew what holdups there might be—my mother hired a car and they drove up together to see the crater and the piles of rubble that were all that was left of the house and of nearby Chelsea Old Church.

No. 74's first tenant after my parents left was the artist James McNeil Whistler, who actually died there in 1903; after him came the sculptor Jacob Epstein. One of his truncated, nude, but still very obviously male figures so shocked my grandmother, who still lived at No. 37, another of the Cheyne Walk houses my father had built, that she is said to have had difficulty looking in its direction.

The last tenant of No. 74 was, in fact, Laurence Olivier, but his wife, Vivien Leigh, was said never to have liked the place. It was standing empty when the land mine destroyed it. Only a few months before, my mother and I had met and been over the house together. She was probably checking as to its condition, for Olivier claimed that since he was now serving in the Fleet Air Arm he could no longer afford to pay the £60 a year rent. Hitler absolved him of that.

Perhaps my mother wanted me to see the first little home she had gone to as a young, very "liberated" married woman. She and I wandered the empty rooms, me incongruous in my WAAF uniform as she reminisced about her life there at the turn of the century and, with her descriptions, peopled it with their friends and visitors. We both decided that the huge bar the Oliviers built—and left behind—was much too big for the scale of the place.

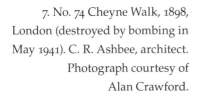

7. No. 74 Cheyne Walk, 1898, London (destroyed by bombing in May 1941). C. R. Ashbee, architect. Photograph courtesy of Alan Crawford.

Barely a month later, a Nazi bomber escaping over Kent jettisoned the last unused bombs of its load—three five-hundred pounders—over our home at Godden Green. They just missed the house but left the garden a series of enormous craters and a tragic tangle of splintered, uprooted trees. The Victorian seesaw that had been my mother's and her young brother's joy in the 1880s, and ours as children in the late 1920s, vanished completely. Even the great weight which could be moved along the central column of the seesaw to equalise the weights of different sizes of children, was never found again. And a strong Victorian iron seat had been thrown up into the air to come down again a tarantula-like ball of screwed-up metal.

But it was the death of the trees that distressed my father even more than the recent destruction of his architectural work. He raged as he stumbled through the broken branches of the stately silver birch, the huge ilex, and the rarer tulip tree.

Shortly before this happened, my sister Mary Lewis had temporarily taken over the role of "daughter at home" with her baby, born just a year earlier in July 1940. The thunder of the bombs brought my mother and Mary Murphy running from their rooms to converge on the upstairs landing, talking excitedly and checking that no one had been hurt by the flying glass. Suddenly Mary emerged from her room. "Shhh!" she said, finger on lips. "You'll wake Olivia!"

Meanwhile, at HQ Fighter Command, changes were taking place too, as increasing numbers of WAAF who had been some time in the ranks got commissions. Two of our Filter Room sergeants, the roly-poly Scots Sadie Younger and the serene, elegantly square-faced blonde Joyce Pearman-Smith, both went for training as Filter officers, the first women to reach this technical pinnacle. They soon came back in their officer's uniforms and now had to be called Ma'am.

My friend Rita got a Code and Cypher commission and was also posted back to the HQ Fighter Command. She discovered that she could find her own billet if she wanted to, and that the Convent was willing to rent her a tiny room. This meant that I could drop in and visit her if off-duty times fitted. But I had no idea what scandal this would lead me in for, on two counts, only one of which was the infringement of the tradition that there should be no "fratting" between Commissioned and Other Ranks!

I was in the Rest Room one day when our solid-bosomed Sergeant Miller, Administrator (Admin), beckoned me. "Come 'ere Ash," she said. "I want a word with you." "What's the trouble, Dusty?" I asked, as I went over to where she was standing. (All Millers are "Dusty," so Dusty was what she was called.)

"Well, Ash, It's all the talk about you and, er, well, you and Rita Beadon."

"What d'you mean . . . talk?"

"Well . . . you and her together like. You know what I mean, Ash."

"What? Because she's an officer now?"

"That doesn't exactly help. But no, I mean, you know . . . lovey-dovey stuff." I burst out laughing.

"Its no laughing matter, Ash, I'm telling you. You better do something about it! Sharpish!"

"But Dusty," I said, suddenly aware I must be serious, "that's plain *crazy!*" She shook her head, but her solemn expression told me that she really meant it. "Pretty sharpish," she repeated.

"But Sarge!" I said, "What on earth am I supposed to *do?* Who's behind this . . . this, slander?" She pulled me towards her large, compact form. "If you ask me, I thinks it's Grogon," she whispered conspiratorially.

"What? Old Grog?"

"No good bein' disrespectful now she's a bloody officer," said Dusty. "If you want my advice, you don't want to let no grass grow under your feet. You go right away and see 'er. Take the bull by the bloody 'orns is what I say!"

"OK, Sarge. I'll do just that. And thanks." And I gave her a mock salute and went off to work out a plan of action. I made an appointment to see S/O Grogon, and having decided as before that attack was the best form of defence, I worked myself up to a pitch of righteous indignation before I knocked on the door.

"Ah yes, Ashbee, you wanted to see me," she said, as I saluted and stood rigidly to attention in front of her.

"Ma'am!" I plunged in. "I've come to protest. There are rumours going round about me apparently . . . I can't *think* where they originate from," I added darkly, "that I'm . . . that I'm having a lesbian affair with A/S/O Beadon."

"Oh, er . . . Ashbee," Grogon was obviously taken aback by my vehemence. I pressed my advantage. In fact by this time genuinely upset, my voice sounded even to me, surprisingly, in fact convincingly, emotional.

"Just because I've got short hair, Ma'am, there's no reason to spread libellous, I mean scandalous suggestions. I've always had short hair and . . ."

"All right, all right, Ashbee, calm down, take it easy. No one's accusing you."

"Yes, but they *are* Ma'am! *That's* what I'm protesting about! It's not fair on me, and it's not fair on Beadon! Just because . . ."

"OK, OK, Ashbee, I take your point. I'll . . ."

"I just wanted to be sure, Ma'am, that if you heard anything, you'd *know* there was absolutely nothing in it. Just because . . ."

"All right, Ashbee. You've made your complaint. Was there anything else?"

"No, Ma'am, thank you, Ma'am." I went back to the Huts and told Sergeant Miller. "Old Grog seemed a bit surprised," I said.

"Like I said," the Sarge commented with a knowing smile. "You 'ave to take the bull by the 'orns. Good for you Ash! That'll 've fixed 'er OK. All the same . . . mark my words, you and Beadon 'ad best be a bit craftier, like." And she winked.

"Now don't you start, you old so-and-so!" I said, "You *know* there's . . ."

"OK, OK, Ash, I was only jokin'."

Such excitements apart, time had to be filled, and the four-hours-on, eight-hours-off system had its limitations. I cast around for other occupations. Before the war I had done some amateur drama with the local village children, and the idea of "putting on a show" grew in my mind. Quite a few members of my watch thought it would be an amusing idea, and several turned out to have hidden talent. I reckoned we could write most of the stuff ourselves. I was advised to go and see the Squadron Leader Admin who was in charge of Station Entertainment.

"So you think you could put on a show, do you Ash?" he said, genially. "Well that sounds OK if you've got enough material to last a whole evening. Got a nice chorus of legs, have you?" He looked with a friendly leer at my lisle stockings. "Singers? Dancers? What? Better go and see Sergeant Freddie Bayco. He's the one to put you on the right track."

Slightly daunted—I had not quite thought in terms of the Folies Bergères, and we had to date written only three short sketches, though other ideas were simmering—I sought out the sergeant. He was a well-known cinema organist, one of that now vanished breed who used to come up and go down by elevator in a rainbow of coloured lights seated at one of those enormous cinema organs so popular in the 1930s.

"OK, Ash, I'm in the picture," he said. "I gather you've written some sketches. Been OK'd yet, have they? Well, just to be on the safe side, you know. You've checked them for time? Three of them, you said? Well, it's a start. So you've an opening and closing chorus, three sketches, a harmony quartet, and a ballet-duet . . ."

"That's a comic stunt," I put in.

"So much the better. But it's not enough. I daresay we can find you a solo pianist somewhere, and a violinist too, for that matter. Oh, and a tap ensemble, you said. Haven't you got a singer?"

"Well," I said dubiously, "I suppose I could . . . at a pinch."

He sat straight down at the piano and played a few chords. "Right. Try you out. What numbers do you know?"

"Numbers?" I said faintly.

"Songs," he said patiently.

"Oh! Songs! Well, I know some Negro Spirituals. Would 'Swing Low, Sweet Chariot' be any good?"

He started playing without further comment or preamble and took me steadily up the scale to the highest note I could comfortably reach. I rather enjoyed it.

"Well," he said swinging himself round the piano stool with an attractive smile. "What you don't know about singing would fill two books, but you'll do. Now, what shall we give you to sing? I know! Chopin's 'So Deep Is the Night.' That's a nice arrangement, and Joyce Kilmer's 'Trees.' That's a very popular number at the moment. Got a pretty frock stowed away somewhere?" he added, glancing not too hopefully at my somewhat solid form.

I nodded. I really had. A beautiful taffeta creation with big checks in navy, grey, and white, and a bouffant sleeve, that I'd hardly ever had a chance to wear.

"Good. Oh, and has the show got a title?"

"*Filtered Fragments,*" I said firmly. We plunged into rehearsals, made easier by the fact that the entire cast was from my own watch, though I had problems dragging sleeping bodies out of bed at odd hours to go through the sketches and dance routines. A rotund little Admin Corporal Blunn was the tap expert and schooled the high kicks of the chorus, as well as playing other minor roles. The head of our watch, Sergeant "Willi" Williams, agreed to be my foil for the mock ballet. She was "petite" and looked just like something out of *Swan Lake* anyway. We rehearsed to a crackling gramophone record of Dvorak's *Arabesque* with someone

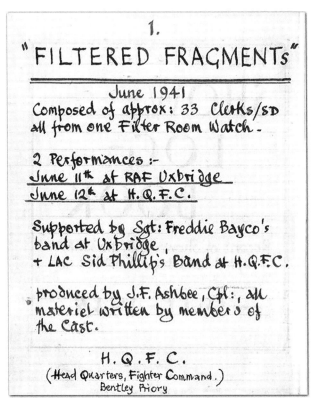

1.

"FILTERED FRAGMENTs"

June 1941
Composed of approx: 33 Clerks/sD
all from one Filter Room Watch.

2 Performances :-
June 11th at RAF Uxbridge
June 12th at H.Q.F.C.

Supported by Sgt: Freddie Bayco's
band at Uxbridge,
+ LAC Sid Phillip's Band at H.Q.F.C.

produced by J.F. Ashbee, Cpl:, all
materiel written by members of
the Cast.

H.Q.F.C.
(Head Quarters, Fighter Command.)
Bentley Priory

8. *Filtered Fragments.* Felicity's notes in her show log book,
on her first show, performed June 1941.

standing in the wings dropping gravel and broken glass out of a bucket
every time I faked dropping my partner. We got it to a fine art.

The sketches were all very topical. One about new recruits, we called
"Raw Bodies." Another was "Kit Inspections" (often a sore point), and my
prize piece was a skit on WAAF Officer Selection Boards. I even got away
with a phrase such as "A naice girl, but not quaite the Officer Taipe." In
fact, in those early days, a good golf handicap was known to be the prime
consideration for getting a WAAF commission.

And then, in the middle of all this unheroic busyness, who should come
dropping in out of the moonlit sky on that night of 10 May 1941, but Hitler's

No. 2, the alleged Deputy Fuehrer, Rudolph Hess! Of course we didn't know it was Hess until the news broke two days later, but in spite of that, surprisingly, I and the Ottercops Moss plotter too, who has been in touch with me since, remember what happened as clearly as if it were yesterday. It was the night of the big London raid when the House of Commons was hit, though we didn't know that at the time either. But there were lulls in the raid. In the sudden stillness of one of them, far out in the empty North Sea, a single counter was put down by the Ottercops Moss plotter.

I had knitted and played chess [during reports from] Ottercops Moss in the early days and well remembered the derision that greeted suggestions that that station had picked up five hundred plus aircraft. It always meant a thunderstorm! Ottercops was one of the first of the CH (Chain Home) stations,[3] sited on high ground about twenty-nine miles northwest of Newcastle (I would later be posted there as an Admin). But there were problems. Something to do with magnetics. They'd even had one of those despised "Scientific Observers" up there trying to sort things out. Now there was a well-suppressed ripple of mirth. Not thunder tonight, surely. Everyone knew it was a full moon, with quite exceptional visibility. But there *was* something odd about it. A single aircraft? Over 150 miles out?

The Ottercops Moss WAAF put down another counter, and soon another. The neighbouring station picked up the signal, and a third. Finally the Filter Officer was forced to take note. He bent over the map and put down his first arrow. I told it through. The lone aircraft flew on, and crossing the coast, left our map for the Ops Room one, where we heard later that the Observer Corps had confirmed it. No more than that until the papers splashed the news, which even at a time of much greater

---

3. The Chain Home radar defensive system was both the first of its kind anywhere and the first to be used in warfare. Developed in the mid-1930s and installed before World War II, its stations initially covered the east and south coasts of Great Britain. Though the system was technically "primitive" compared to advances in radar design that arrived during the war, it nonetheless contributed crucially to British defenses during the Battle of Britain. Part of the effectiveness of Chain Home came from its Control and Reporting system. Felicity Ashbee began her WAAF career within that system. For a history of Chain Home see Jack Gough, *Watching the Skies* (London: HMSO, 1993).

reticence and secrecy could not be concealed. Even in the *Times* it made exciting reading.

The Scots ploughman David Maclean "rounded up" the injured parachutist seen dropping from his crashing plane. The Foreign Office official, who had once met Hess, was hurriedly flown up to identify him in the hospital where he had been taken because of his broken ankle. Then came Churchill's statement in the House. Rumour had it that "Big Names" were involved, the Duke of Hamilton's amongst them. Our canteen buzzed with the thought of fascinating scandals.

And then the story faded, for there was no television to hype things up with constant visual details, and radio reports were often discreetly worded and extremely guarded. Anyway, bigger events were already looming on the horizon. And for our watch particularly, that meant THE SHOW!

I was soon enlightened by a jazz fan about Sid Phillips. "You can't mean *the* Sid Phillips. You mean he and his group are going to *improvise* for your mock ballet? Just like that? Crikey!"

"Well, yes. That's what Sergeant Bayco said."

"What, *Freddie* Bayco?"

I blinked owlishly. "Well, yes."

"*Crikey!*"

Which I interpreted as meaning we ought to get a good audience at both shows. We had only one run-through with Sid Phillips and his band. We had managed to get a real tutu for Willi to wear, and I had a pair of emerald green, woollen "Long-Johns." Sold as under-ski pants, they were the most daring thing out at a time when underwear was always supposed to be white, or at most, a pastel shade. With a flimsy white blouse I managed to convey a faintly Anton Dolin-ish impression, in spite of my solidity.

Sid Phillips killed himself laughing and knew exactly what was needed. "You just carry right on the way you've worked it out. No need to change anything. We've got it all buttoned up. We'll just follow you, back you up, improvise. No problem. It'll go down great!" And it did. In fact the whole performance did. Except for one thing. I simply could not memorize the words of that absolutely terrible number, "Trees." Yet there I stood, in my elegant party frock, spotlighted in front of an audience of six hundred or so, and sang:

I think that I shall never see
A poem lovely as a tree
A tree whose hungry mouth is pressed
Against the earth's sweet flowing breast . . .

No, No! Surely I must have got it wrong! Breasts don't *flow!* They may *over*flow, if not entirely contained. The WAAF variant was usually well squared-up by tunic breast pockets filled with AF Identity Papers, illicit powder compacts, and other things that gas masks failed to accommodate, but not *flow!* With a hint of panic I hurried on and launched myself into the second verse. It sounded no more idiotic than usual.

I think that I shall never wear
A nest of robins in my hair
whose bosom snow was lain (whose? the robin's?)
Who intimately lives with rain (Who . . . *Who?*)
Poems are made by *gods* like me (crescendo)
But only *fools,* can make . . . a . . . TRE-E-E-E.

The applause was deafening. I honestly believe nobody noticed anything odd about the lunacy of the words. They must just have liked the sound. I acknowledged the thunder of issue Air Force boots blushingly, managing not to trip over my long frock as I left the stage.

A few days later, though it can have had nothing to do with it, I was summoned to the Orderly Room and told fill out a form and apply for a commission. I was in two minds about this. On the one hand, my old instincts were to remain on the "correct," i.e., the *left* side of the Barricades, "Come the Revolution!" On the other hand, I was increasingly restive with so little opportunity to take responsibility for my own or anyone else's actions. Surely I might be able to be of more *use* to the war effort as an officer.

"What sort of a commission?" I parried.

"Intelligence. You've got some languages haven't you?"

I admitted it, somewhat warily.

"Well . . . then . . ." So I filled out the papers and within a week or two found myself at another overgrown RAF-rented "hideout," this time near Gerrards Cross. Revolution or no, my days in the ranks were ended.

PART 2

The Officer Type? (Commissioned)

June 1941–February 1944

4. Intelligence
1941–1942

WHATEVER VAGUE AND ROMANTIC IDEAS might have been floating through my mind at the thought of an Intelligence Commission (Blonde spies? Secret agents? My foreign languages used in some unexpectedly exciting way?), they quickly faded as I humped my kitbag into the spacious hall of yet another respectable Stockbroker Tudor suburban-rural house.

The bedrooms were big enough to squeeze in four or five RAF beds (even embryo officers had to share), and the rug-skidding, parquet-floored drawing room offered standard armchairs and sofas upholstered in recognizably conservative floral prints. Here we assembled before and after meals, learning to behave like Officers and Gentlemen, after the crudities of Other Ranks life. It was a mixed-sex Officer Training fortnight, but the image was still of the Gentleman. What was now an improvised classroom (there was even a blackboard) had probably once been a fairly extensive library, and here we had the lectures deemed necessary to mould the Officer Type and give both men and women what, at the time, were thought to be the necessary rudiments of administration and leadership.

"Ah, Ashbee. Let's see now. You're Code and Cypher?"

"No, Sir, Intelligence, Sir."

"Intelligence? . . . Ah, well, er, there don't seem to be any, er . . . Well, I'd just sit at the back and listen."

It turned out to be a very hot fortnight, and as the lectures about equipment or administration problems droned on, the open French windows gave tantalizing glimpses of the overgrown and neglected garden just made for truanting.

"Ah, Ashbee, let's see, was it, er . . . Catering?"

"No, Sir, Intelligence, Sir."

"Intelligence, Ashbee? Oh, I don't think . . . er."

"I'll just sit at the back Sir, shall I?"

"Yes, yes, Ashbee, you do that."

So I sat at the back, twiddling my thumbs, thinking my own thoughts, and on one occasion being summoned to be measured for my officer's uniform. The gentlemen's tailor was obviously as yet unused to feminine bust measurements, let alone the problem of where to stop when going down a female leg to calculate correct skirt lengths. He simply could not make a lady kneel before him.

The rule-of-thumb method used by WAAF Officers with female Other Ranks was that when kneeling, the hem should just touch the ground.

My bedroom stable-companions were hardly kindred spirits, but one of them complained one morning of having been bitten during the night. "It couldn't be fleas, could it?" she asked, aghast.

I looked at the large blotched bites sympathetically, and with the expertise of my Jerusalem childhood, pronounced verdict: "That's not fleas! That's bugs!"

"What do you mean . . . bugs?"

"Bedbugs, of course!" There was a shriek of horror and the others gathered round. "Never met a bedbug before?" I asked, rather enjoying the shock value of my greater experience. "We'd better have a look in your bed." (A gasp of embarrassment.) "They're easy to catch, they don't jump like fleas. On the other hand they usually come out only at night when the bed's nicely warmed up." (Another suppressed shriek.)

I went through the bedclothes carefully, watched by my fascinated but ignorantly ladylike companions. "Ha! *got* 'im!" I exclaimed, pouncing on the small, dark, flat culprit. "Quick, a matchbox somebody . . . tip the matches out, quick!"

"What are you going to *do?*" came in chorus.

"Take it down and complain, of course. You'd better come too," I turned to the bitten victim, "and show off your bites."

"Oh, I couldn't!" the shocked response.

"Up to you," I said, shrugging, "But I don't think it's good enough. We didn't bring bedbugs with us, wherever we may have come from recently. It is supposed to be officer training here!"

My cap on, to show a proper deference, and matchbox in hand, I went down to the WAAF Admin Officer's holy of holies, knocked, and went in. Saluting smartly I lodged my complaint, to be met by a stony disbelief. "The bitten victim was too shy to come and display her bites, Ma'am," I said, "though that is not essential, since I have caught and can show you the offender."

A second's doubt—or panic?—flickered across the face of the Senior WAAF as I produced my matchbox. But I had forgotten the wiles of the enemy. A cake of wetted soap clapped on a flea is the easy way to imprison that lively little menace, but a bedbug can squeeze its small flat, black, ace-of-spades-shaped body in or out of anything not hermetically sealed. The matchbox was empty.

Perhaps they shouldn't have picked me for Intelligence after all? But they had, so I went on taking my seat unobtrusively in the back row. It was, if nothing else, a much-needed rest after months of busy night watches. There was one lecture, though, which had me instantly alert and which I have never forgotten. A solid, dark-haired man, obviously a historian stuffed reluctantly into an RAF uniform, but patently an expert of no mean order, gave a prophetic analysis of the Russians' paranoid fear of attack, and of their attempts at guarding, by fair means or foul, the several "gateways" into Mother Russia.

The speaker may even have had "inside information," for it is thought that Hess knew the Nazi attack on the Soviet Union was imminent when he arrived in Britain on that night of 10 May. I can still see the lecturer's diagrams, with locations and names of many of those gateways.

By the time I reached my first posting, Station X, as a fully fledged if totally untrained and ignorant Intelligence Officer, the Nazis were already well into mainland Russia, and the feared and hated Soviets were now our allies. The Russian national anthem was added to the list of the anthems of other invaded countries. Standing to attention must have stuck in the gullet of many a Regular.

Station X was in fact Bletchley Park, and in 1941 it was a dump. As far I was concerned, absolutely the only "advantage"—and it was a very marginal one—was that if I went anywhere, and signing-in was necessary, it was quite fun to write Station X. But there was no station as such, and there seemed to be no rhyme or reason why some people were in Army uniforms, others in Air Force or Naval ones, while a huge number were in "civvies." I merely had to report to my WAAF Officer Admin in charge. I was then shown in which Nissen hut I would be working and given the address of my billet.

Of course in true British fashion it was all wrapped in mystery anyway, and I only learned bit by bit that my "top boss" was one of the renowned code-crackers, Josh Cooper. He would sometimes breeze into our office, stand for a moment, his right hand fumbling round the back of his head with its shock of little boy's dark hair, and grab his left ear, a prelude to some intricate question which I was terrified might one day be directed at me. But it was usually tossed, head not turned in my direction, at my more immediate superior, a neat, dapper, bespectacled civilian by the name of "Bonzo." He and Diana, a pale, quiet girl, probably a few years older than myself, shared an office, though I have no idea what either of them was really working at.

People without proper names or even identities were occasionally glimpsed in the canteen, and it was hinted with a nudge that they were from "the other side," which, being interpreted, meant the Secret Service proper. They never even paid income tax, I was told, for fear of their being traced. If the whole place hadn't struck gloom in my heart from day one, I might have been mildly amused at having landed somewhere so *top* secret after my brush only a year ago with whatever department was hunting Reds-under-the-bed.

I had absolutely no idea what I was supposed to be doing but was offered sheaves of paper which I was told were the conversations of German pilots logged by "our girls" at listening stations on the coast. I had to go through these to see if there were any lapses of security, any uncoded words or half-sentences, that might help identify which stations the aircraft were operating from.

Alas, for the poor girls taking it all down, and for me having to wade through it, the German pilots' security seemed to be impregnable. On sheet after sheet after sheet, they were "circling the red beacon" or the green one, or giving a height unrelated to any previous or subsequent remark, or anything at all that could have given a fix on them. The occasional gaps and lines of dots on the log sheets, due to bad weather or momentary radar failure, were slight visual relief, but no help.

The quiet Diana turned out to be either the daughter or niece of the Russian expert and writer Bernard Pares, and she may well have been trying to befriend me. But as Bletchley offered no reasonable place to meet, there was no social life worth the name. True, there was one café with two or three wobbly tables and half a dozen cane chairs, their basketry painted a seasick green, lightly brushed with "old gold." Here, bangers-and-mash and cups of tea could be had, but it was hardly a place to start a friendship, and any interesting conversation would have been stillborn. In any case, most people went home to their billets, where the evening meal was provided free in the contract.

George and Margaret Britten, on whose door I knocked on that first evening at Station X, lived in a brick semidetached house built some five years before with the £500 compensation George got in for an accident at work. He was a labourer at Flettons Brickworks, one of the Bletchley's main employers, and had been inside one of the machines cleaning it when someone inadvertently switched it on. He was nearly turned into a brick, lost several fingers and his spine was broken; they doubted he would ever walk again. But they didn't know George! When I lived with them, he was doing a twelve-hour day at the brickworks, though he was a little wary of the machines.

The house, with a sizeable garden at the back, was their pride and joy. It had a bathroom with a gas geyser to heat the water. Unfortunately the jerry-builder had forgotten the toilet, and this had had to be added on outside at the back of the house as a sudden afterthought and had not been wired for light. It was one of the purgatories of that bitter winter (Buckinghamshire is cold country at the best of times) to have to scurry outside last thing, with my torch in my mouth, to use it.

But on those first summer evenings I would cycle back from my boring log-watch to find George, having already eaten his cooked tea, out in the garden hard at work in the vegetable patch. Digging for Victory was in full swing by then, and everyone with a bit of garden or an allotment was being exhorted to forget the flowers and plant more vegetables. We were soon heartily tired of carrots, but onions were worth their weight in gold! A prima donna somewhere was alleged to have been overjoyed when on taking her curtain call she was offered not a bouquet of flowers, but a bunch of onions.

George had planted some that seemed to be doing very well, and he had me out in the garden more than once to see how they were coming along. At last they were ready to pull up, but Sunday after Sunday passed (no lesser meal than Sunday dinner could properly be graced by George's prized onions), and we never had them.

At last I plucked up courage to mention it to Margaret. "Aren't we ever going to eat George's onions?" I asked. "But there isn't any steak!" she wailed. Apparently steak-and-onions was the only way that she and George could envisage eating these prized vegetables. And then, mercifully, one of Margaret's brothers took George out shooting, and they got a rabbit. Although this was very much second best, the onions had not yet gone mouldy and were used to ennoble the humble alternative.

With Double Summer Time George would be out in the garden till nearly eleven, when the light began to fade. He would then come in for "supper," a cup of cocoa made with water topped with a drop of milk and a bit of bread and cheese. He was up again at five the next morning and off on his bike to the brickworks.

It must have been around midsummer that Bonzo threw something new at me. "Here, Ash, you've got some Russian, haven't you? Take a look at this stuff, will you? It's suddenly started coming in. Seems as if there are some freak weather conditions which are giving what the Radar wallahs call a double-bounce. You probably know about that? 'Our Girls' have been picking up tank-to-tank conversations right out in the Minsk Smolensk areas, not possible normally. Could you make a map of the place-names mentioned at the same time and report on it?"

At last something interesting! I started off by making a map of eastern Europe and western Russia which presented only minor problems, and pushing the alarming word "report" to the back of my mind, concentrated on identifying place-names that occurred in the log sheets, and entering them on the map. The logged conversations, though often scrappy and difficult to make sense of, whether in German or Russian, seemed fascinatingly immediate.

To a very partial initiate like myself, and in very unscientific terms, what appeared to be happening was that radar pulses were going up, hitting one of the "layers" (I could never remember the difference between the "heavy side" [Heaviside layer] or the "Appleton layer"), coming down again, bouncing off again for another jab at one of the layers and coming down yet again as chance would have it, in the area of Russia being attacked by the Nazis.[1] Since the earth's surface is curved and radar pulses could not bend, such an extraordinary direct contact between the coasts of Norfolk or Essex or Byelorussia could, it seemed, only occur by means of the "double-bounce" Bonzo referred to.

There was something almost uncanny about the thought that a WAAF sitting in a little mobile van in a meadow in England could be picking up the voices of Germans, talking to each other in their tanks, in Russia, during a war, and actually hear one saying to another: "Look out! There's a Russian over there by that tree. I'm not sure if he's dead or alive."

The freak weather conditions, if that's what really had caused the phenomenon, lasted about six weeks; then the transmissions stopped as suddenly as they had begun. But a Fine Arts training followed by a bit of square-bashing, and a stint of Special Duties, had hardly fitted me to write reports for code-cracking Boffins.[2] I didn't know where to begin, and thankfully handed over the results of my research to Bonzo to do what he could with it. For me it was back to ". . . height 9,000 . . . circling Red Beacon . . ."

---

1. The Kennelly Heaviside Layer, discovered in 1924 by physicists Oliver Heaviside and Arthur Kennelly, postulated the existence of a layer of ionized gas in the upper atmosphere capable of reflecting radio waves upward for a distance of 60 to 90 miles. In 1926 Edward V. Appleton discovered another layer 150 miles above sea level, electronically stronger and able to reflect short waves around the earth. Both discoveries were important to the development of radar. See *Nobel Lectures, Physics 1942–1962* (Amsterdam: Elsevier Publishing Co., 1964).

2. Experts.

In spite of my earnest but fumbling efforts and the Anglo-Russian agreement of mutual assistance signed in July in Moscow, the Germans swept on, and by September the Siege of Leningrad had begun.

———————•———————

Obviously the only thing to relieve the boredom of Bletchley Park was to put on another show, so I went the rounds digging out WAAF, Airmen, and Army types with a bit of talent and enough interest to give up some evenings in the NAAFI[3] or the local pub and come to rehearsals. We soon mustered a motley but friendly collection of thirty-six bodies. There were WAAF and WREN teleprinter operators, various Army Police types and a Pioneer Corps Private Crayston with a very tolerable tenor voice.

Again we wrote a good deal of the material ourselves, and we based one "sketch" on the idea of a handful of people from different parts of the country, caught in a shelter during a raid. The show, called *Blue and Khaki*, was to take place in mid-December. The Germans had taken Kharkov in October [1941] and were starting their second offensive against Moscow. The proceeds of our efforts were to go to the Tanks for Russia Fund. There had been a Russian Tank Week in September in which every British arms factory had taken part.

A week before the show, the Japanese attacked Pearl Harbor, and the Americans finally came into the war. So it was an emotional moment which I was ready to make use of, even though Yanks would not yet be a part of it. The sketch gave a chance for everyone in it either to sing or tell their own bomb story, and I decided to coach our Pioneer Corps tenor in a couple of Russian songs, in Russian, and make him appear in a white Cossack costume as a sort of apparition in the shelter.

This costume had been brought back from the Caucasus before World War I by my uncle, Nevill Forbes, professor of Russian at Oxford. It had a row of cartridge cases across the chest, a tall, dramatic, white caracul cap, and damascene sword, which our tenor sitting on his bed spent hours

3. Navy, Army, Air Force Institutes, equivalent in some ways to the American Military Post Exchange (PX) systems.

polishing. This he drew from its scabbard with such relish that I feared there might be casualties in the extremely cramped conditions of the Bletchley Village Hall stage.

The next problem was how to achieve a dramatic enough lighting effect. We desperately needed a dimmer. And here the little RAF Corporal who had volunteered to help with the lights came up trumps. "Easy!" he said. "All you want is one of them big washstand jugs. I'll bring mine from the billet. Me landlady won't mind. You just fill it with water, and put the ends in . . ."

"Ends?" I said faintly. "What ends?"

"Flex," he replied patiently.

"Naked ends?" I was aghast. "I thought electricity and water . . ."

He smiled sweetly. "You just leave it to me, Ma'am. Don't worry. But perhaps better don't look neither."

He was right, of course. At the crucial moment, the lights began to dim and suddenly there was Private Crayston. He was transfigured, Russian pouring from his lips (even those Boffins present from the Slavonic section were quite impressed). As he flashed his damascened blade out of its scabbard on a crescendo, up came the lights again, added to by myself beaming a torch with a bit of red tissue paper over it on him from the wings. I steeled myself for a glance at my lighting expert. And there he was, crouched over a splendid patterned Victorian washstand jug, carefully manipulating his two bits of flex in and out of the water with a seraphic smile on his face.

The Cossack's appearance was the highlight of the evening; it evoked a special round of applause, and I heard afterwards that Private Crayston's rendering of those two Russian songs became quite a hit at the local pubs—even without the swish of the damascene blade or the caracul headgear!

During the working hours, though, I did have the occasional break from the circling Red Beacons. The high-ups must have begun to worry that British pilots' security didn't really match up to the German variety, so from time to time a watch was kept on our own boys in the air. The results were not too reassuring. On some days I found myself reading not German Ground to Air and Air to Ground, but our own boys giving things away left, right, and centre. Code words can be easily compromised if used in too close proximity with ordinary phrases. "Baby" was at one time the code word for a convoy, probably a bit too obvious in any case. But when a pilot cheerfully says, "Where's your baby? Mine's going north," that's the end of that code word, and it had better be realized quickly.

I remember another such instance of the gorgeous irresponsibility of our imaginative and spontaneous pilots.

"Joy" at one time meant having shot down an enemy aircraft.

Ground to Air: "Had any joy today?"

Air to Ground: "No, but I had a bloody ecstasy yesterday."

There was also the risk that the sheer amount of continuous speaking helped the enemy to get a fix on the aircraft concerned; it could then be homed in on and shot down. Silence in the air, though lonely, could be golden. Somebody suggested that a pocket-sized, illustrated booklet of a humorous nature might encourage pilots to be more security-conscious and could be worth trying. I was given the job of designing it, an assignment after my own heart.

9. *The Hun Tunes In.* Felicity's original proposal for the cover of the security booklet, designed while stationed at Station X, 1942. Ink, pencil, and colored pencil on paper (not published).

But maybe it was thought that such a booklet, if found on a captured airman, might be as damaging as their cheerful lack of security in the air, for it never appeared. Instead I was disgusted to see a short article in the internal RAF magazine, using some of my ideas and pictures of Hitler-Mädchen giving the Nazi salute as they handed over compromised code words to their superiors.[4] They had all been redrawn by the "resident artist". I was thankful my name hadn't been used. It confirmed my feeling that it wouldn't be worth bothering trying to launch my idea that Cockney rhyming slang would be the one thing to fox German code-crackers. Its sheer irrationality would have kept their serious noses in card indexes "for the duration."

In May 1942 my father died, and I got compassionate leave to go down to Kent for the funeral. I stayed on for a week to help my mother and sister Mary with the huge problem of dealing with the house [at Godden Green] and [its] contents. The immediate task was to get the place ready for takeover by the Military, who had requisitioned it. The usual procedure in such cases was for the house to be cleared with the exception of one room into which everything the family wished to keep would be stuffed, after which the doors would be ceremoniously sealed until such time as the Military gave up possession. In our case, this meant dealing with my father's library of approximately nine thousand books. A rare-books dealer came down to take stock of it, since my father had never got around to making a proper catalogue.

The dealer was a gentle, grey-haired, professional type who went quietly on with his listing while the rest of us milled round him trying to decide about whatever furniture to keep, against an impossible to imagine "after the war" situation. Who would be living where, and with whom, if they survived, or if the house survived? For my mother, after forty-four years of married life, sorting it all out physically, let alone emotionally, kept her mercifully busy.

4. *TEE EMM* 12 (March 1942): 20–24. The article redrew nearly all of Ashbee's sketches and used her text almost verbatim.

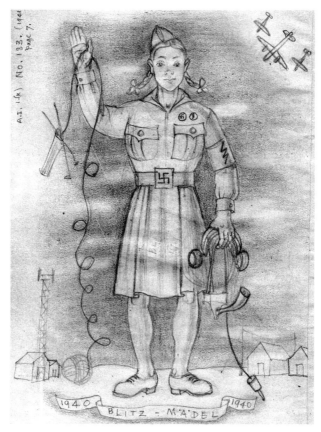

10. Detail from Felicity's security booklet proposal. Pencil and colored pencil on paper.

Arrangements for a sale of the surplus furniture was by no means simple either, for the petrol rationing was at its most stringent and it was doubtful how many people would want to use this precious commodity driving to a country sale. Also raids continued, and the wailing sirens were a perpetual reminder that what man (or in this case woman) might propose, other "forces" might easily dispose.

In any event, a few antique-dealing rings arranged things between them, and mahogany tallboys with huge mirrors, the oak dining room table with a dozen leaves to add in for family gatherings, even some

1942   TEE EMM

Again, suppose you are out on a sweep over France.

You meet a bunch of 109s and get separated from your formation in the ensuing dogfights.

When it's all over you switch on your R/T and tell your section leader that you have shot down a 109 over, say, Bethune, that you have used up all your ammunition and so are making for home *via* Hardelot.

Sounds harmless enough.

But the Germans concentrate pretty hard on cutting off stragglers from sweeps and those few words of yours may have made all the difference to your chances of getting home.

This is how the Germans run their Listening Service.

First, they set up a series of small wireless receiving stations along the French, Belgian and Dutch coasts, so that their range includes as large an area of England as possible. Each of these small stations will man enough receivers to cover all the R/T frequencies they wish to hear, and they will maintain a twenty-four-hour watch.

WE KNOW THAT THEY EMPLOY GIRLS AS RADIO OPERATORS FOR THIS SERVICE,

21

11. A page from *TEE EMM* magazine, March 1942, illustrated with copies of Felicity's security book drawings.

Chippendale chairs, all went for a song. But at last, the room that was to contain what we had decided to keep was filled up. It included several hundred books that we could not bring ourselves to part with, and the sealing ceremony took place. The Army moved in, and my mother started from camp to camp in the wake of my sister Mary and her child.

I went back to Bletchley Park to throw myself into rehearsals for a second show, *Blue and Khaki No. 2*. I also found I had to move my billet. My nice Margaret Britten had a miscarriage, and though I managed to help her through it, and cook for George while she was incapacitated, she felt she couldn't cope, and I moved to another "Pride and Joy" house. But here the bathroom (with toilet!) was *so* sacred that it was seldom allowed to be used, for fear of condensation spoiling the beautiful glossy pink paint.

So I moved again, to a much more congenial environment. Mr. and Mrs. Ramsbotham ran a huge market garden, and I remember being amused by the instructions he had received about how much acreage to devote to the particular kind of pink beet (I think it was to be used as "crystallized cherries" in the traditional Dundee-type fruit cake). It was amazing how few people realized they were no longer eating the real thing. The little round bits *looked* the same.

By this time, though, I had decided to ask my Senior WAAF officer if there was any way of extricating myself from the boredom of "Intelligence." She was one of the daughters of the famous child psychiatrist Dr. Creighton-Miller, and she had a delightfully raucous laugh.

"Well, Ash, what do you want instead? Not Code and Cypher, surely? I can't see you in Equipment or Accountancy either!"

"God, no!" I said. "I think I'd be more use in Administration."

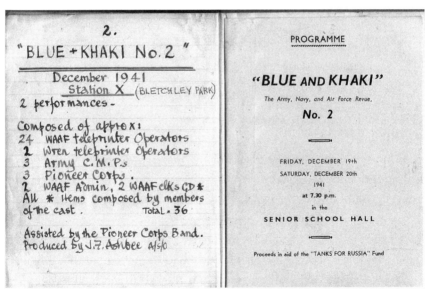

12. *Blue and Khaki No. 2.* Felicity's notes and the printed program cover from her show log book. Blue and red ink on paper. December 1941.

13. *Shuddering Heights*, "The prison-cells of 'Narcisse' and 'Ladislaus.'" As first performed at RAF Station X, Bletchley Park, 29–30 May 1942.

14. *Shuddering Heights*, "Bibi: 'Sh! The revelry is at its height but ere the Hall clock strikes midnight— we will be avenged!' Lolo: 'Sh! Till the hour approaches, let us conceal ourselves in the conservatory!'" As first performed at RAF Station X, Bletchley Park, 29–30 May 1942.

15. *Shuddering Heights*, "'Count' Stenograffski (Ladislaus) & the 'Marquis de la Merdators' (Narcisse) on their way to the Heights." As first performed at RAF Station X, Bletchley Park, 29–30 May 1942.

16. *Shuddering Heights*, Aspidistra and Marmaduke. "Marmaduke: 'May I be forever disgraced, if a hair on my little sister's head be disarranged.'" As first performed at RAF Station X, Bletchley Park, 29–30 May 1942.

She laughed again. "It's the first time I've ever heard of anyone wanting to transfer *out* of Intelligence. Is it really as boring as all that?" I nodded, and she said vociferously, "Well, we'll see what we can do. Actually, I think you'd be rather good as Admin." It took a couple of months.

I filled my time with the new show. Its pièce de résistance was *Shuddering Heights,* a mock Victorian melodrama I had written for family use some years before. It had lovely costumes, two escaped convicts, two "ladies of easy virtue" (Lola and Bibi), and a heroine called Aspidistra Shudderbottom. At the end everyone was dead on the stage. It went down big!

Sometime afterwards, my transfer came through. I said good-bye to Station X with a light heart in spite of some good friends I had made there and got my self, my bicycle, and my kitbag onto the train to Loughborough for a month's Admin course.

5. A/S/O Admin
1942

THE LOUGHBOROUGH COURSE was almost totally unmemorable, apart from the fact that it was in the purpose-built premises of the new Loughborough Training College, which had a swimming pool with one glass wall. This was startlingly rare at that date, and as a keen diver I spent as much time as I could using it.

This course too, as well as the one that had made an officer of me, was a rest cure of a kind, as there were no exams at the end of the retraining month. I merely got my posting instructions and with my kitbag and bicycle made the circuitous train journey to Andover in Hampshire to report to RAF Middle Wallop.

It was August, and the Desert War was already rolling backwards and forwards over the sands of North Africa. "Monty" [Field Marshall Bernard Montgomery] had just been given control of the Eighth Army, and the names Tobruk and El Alamein were becoming known points on the map for many whose knowledge of geography had hitherto been minimal. At the same time, in spite of heavy losses, British convoys were battling their way through to Archangel in the far north of Russia. The Germans were losing in Stalingrad.

Middle Wallop was, as you might imagine, between two others of the same name, Over Wallop and Nether Wallop, both of which were mentioned in the Domesday Book. It had been a peacetime RAF station with a full complement of permanent, brick-built barracks. These, with the airfield itself, were on one side of the main road, while on the other were the solid, 1930s-style Officers Mess and a number of married quarters.

In 1942 Middle Wallop was a Fighter-Bomber station operating a rather curious combination of aircraft working in pairs. These were an armed DB-7 Turbinlite Havoc (actually an American plane) equipped with a

68

searchlight in its nose which was turned on as soon as it was fairly sure it had an enemy in its sights. Its hidden partner, a single-seater fighter, then swooped into the attack out of the darkness onto the enemy in the search-light's glare. It was a strange and rather beautiful sight to see the sudden, disembodied beam of light switch itself on, out of nowhere, in the dark sky to catch and hold the enemy plane, a helpless tiny object seeking by desperate evasive action to drop out of the lethal light and avoid instant destruction. But apparently it did not always turn out quite as intended, and the system never became widespread.

The squadron's pilots flying Mosquitoes were for part of the time a bunch of Canadians. They were housed at a pub called The Pheasant, a short distance away from the camp, while we WAAF officers filled several of the married quarters. I found myself sharing a room with one Joyce McFadden, a WAAF Catering Officer, a fairly newish breed amongst com-missioned WAAF, as were Accounts Officers. We went over to the big main building for all meals.

The majority of the WAAF Other Ranks and Airmen lived in the bar-racks that in peacetime had accommodated the unmarried men. They had their own dining rooms and the usual NAAFI where they could pay for platefuls of baked beans and chips to make up the deficiencies of the stan-dard issue food, or just sit in the evenings over extended cups of tea.

At least it was warm in the winter and, to many, not unbearably squalid. In addition to this camp accommodation, two large houses had been taken over for use as hostels for the Clerks S/D who worked shifts in the station's Operations Room. Garlogs, the nearer and smaller of these two houses, was entirely filled by a couple of these Special Duties watches. The main house's history dated back to the early fourteenth century. The building taken over by the RAF was a comfortable, friendly, three-storied house built in 1841, with a terrace and stone steps leading to the front door which was graced by a Doric portico. Behind the house stretched a largish garden dotted with bits of statuary. Here the girls could rest and sunbathe in seclusion. There was even a sizeable fish pond as well as a walled kitchen garden.

The snags were: no easy access to the NAAFI where cigarettes and minor items of toiletry could be had (and very occasionally other rare luxuries). Nor of course was there access to MEN! But since the male Other Ranks actually living on the camp were not the kind that Clerks S/D (still mainly recruited from the so-called upper classes) wanted to associate with anyway, this unsolved conundrum did not have quite the mileage that it might have done. The really determined amongst the girls always managed to get their time off, and the correct passes, to go away with the officers they had set their sights on. In general, "authority" felt it wiser to turn a blind eye.

The other house, called Bossington, is shown on the 1086 Domesday map, though the existing structure, a huge and splendid edifice with shaped gables and tall chimney stacks, dated only from 1834. It stood in romantically palatial grounds through which ran the famous trout river, the Test. Here too, on their rest days after night shifts, the WAAF could roam at their ease in the privacy of the garden, now rapidly going back to a natural state.

I was, as it were, in charge of the WAAF in these two hostels and had to cycle over from time to time to check that everything was ticking over as it should be and that no even minor vandalism was occurring in the imposing rooms. Bossington was quite a longish bicycle ride, and I would be ready for a cup of tea when I swept in past the lodge to be greeted by the tall and beautiful Corporal Admin who lived there and exercised a firm but worldly-wise control over her not always docile flock of fifty or so WAAF.

A bicycle was an indispensable part of a WAAF officer's equipment. Mine was quite a fancy affair with a three-speed gear of which I was very proud, and a dynamo as a lighting system. I had also fixed a small model aircraft onto the front mudguard. At Station X I had sported a Union Jack sprouting up out of a tiny plane's cockpit; as soon as the Germans invaded the Soviet Union and the Russians became our allies, I quickly added a red flag as well.

So as the evenings darkened, I was easily identifiable, bearing down on the Guardroom at top speed. The barrier would be raised with a salute of greeting as I shot through, my cap on the back of my head and my top button undone. This was a highly irregular dress-style, and how I got away with it through the war I sometimes wonder. All fighter pilots kept their top buttons undone; they also had flashy scarves tied like cravats round their necks. I did not go as far as the cravat, but an undone top button was part of my not so hidden protest. If pilots could, why shouldn't I? Regarding the angle of my cap and its hair-coverage, the only times I compromised were when I found myself leading a formal parade.

I was now quite good at these parades and at giving at the exact moment the right words of command in ringing tones. I had been long enough in the ranks to have learned how to paralyze an inefficient WAAF officer marching in front of us. I simply continued to move forward if the officer did not give the command at the correct split second. A platoon of determined women, especially if by any chance they thought they had a grievance, could be pretty intimidating, simply mowing a WAAF officer down or jostling her out of the way. Anyone incapable of moving bodies about by parade-ground words of command was considered fair game.

My other duties as a junior WAAF Admin Officer on a station such as this were pleasantly different from the monotonous checking of German pilots' security-conscious conversations at Bletchley Park. The caring side of what was really personnel management appealed to me immediately as much more interesting. A lot of the WAAF were very young, and many from humbler origins had never been away from home before and desperately needed sympathetic understanding, even some kind of guidance. I soon started a card index system on which I recorded quite a lot of information useful to me personally to keep track of the women and girls I was trying to look after.

By a curious chance, the Admin Officer in charge of Entertainments turned out to be the same Squadron Leader Seymour whose permission I had had to get to put on my first variety show at HQ Fighter Command. It was nice to see a face I knew, still as good-looking and as susceptible to the opposite sex as he had been then.

"Good God! ASH!" he said, on my first appearance in the Mess. "You again? What are you doing here? I thought they were giving you an Intelligence Commission. Didn't they?"

"Yes, Sir! They did, Sir! But I couldn't stand it! Too boring! I got myself transferred."

"Good God! *From* Intelligence? Don't believe it! Or was it just that there weren't any beautiful Nazi pilots to interrogate, what? But, Intelligence

17. Officer Ashbee instructing her WAAF charges in "civics." 1942.

boring? That's good, that is. Well come and have a drink on it! What'll it be? Gin and lime?"

I shuddered. "I'd rather have a whisky, Sir, straight, if I may, Sir?"

"Coming on, what?" he said, with a hint of the old lecherous leer, and a quick glance at my still solid, lisle-stockinged legs. "Want to put another show on here, do you Ash?"

"I might when I've got the hang of things," I answered. "But first, could I do a mural on the wall of the Other Ranks canteen? Liven it up a bit? It's rather bare and, err, drab."

"Mural?" he said. "You mean . . . a painting? What *of?* Nude ladies, perhaps?" This was accompanied by a friendly nudge.

"Well, no, Sir. I thought, actually, er . . . just cooks in cookin' hats, tossing omelettes, or sausages, or something. It wouldn't cost much," I added hurriedly.

"Well, I can't see why not," he said amiably. "Get what you need in the way of paint and bring the chits to me."

So when my WAAF superiors (there were several of them) didn't need me, and nothing more urgent called, I went round to the canteen, got out my pots and brushes, mounted my ladder, and went on with my cooks tossing sausages. I decided to use a fairly simple, almost linear technique, no great areas of oil paint, just distemper straight onto the white-washed walls.

You could still buy loose powder colours in hardware stores in those days, dispensed with a small shovel from little wooden drawers by reluctant assistants in brown overalls, sometimes with a groan because of the mess. I was used to such methods from having done scenery painting. Of course you had to mix up a smelly brew of size, so that it didn't all rub off immediately—it was long before the days of easy emulsion paint, not to forget—but that was no great problem. There were some amused comments, but the fully clothed, sausage-tossing cooks at least cheered things up a bit.[1]

And there were of course other duties as well. Such as Kit Inspections (I was now at the inspecting end instead of standing ramrod straight beside my bed with kit laid out, hoping deficiencies would not be noticed), and the much more dubious Duty Officer Meal Inspections. You had to go round uselessly asking whether the dinner was enjoyable and then stand by the swill-bins to see how much uneaten food was scraped off the plates into them by each Airman or Airwoman as they left the dining room.

The diet of the nation (or at least a large section of that nation) had, in the prewar years, been very restricted, and the average erk, whether the male or female variety, was quite unwilling to experiment with anything that it didn't instantly recognize.

"What the 'ell's that?" or "Don't fancy *that!*" were common reactions to any innovation on the part of the long-suffering catering staff. At one moment there had been a shortage of potatoes and a sudden purchase of turnips. It may well have been one of my stable-companion Joyce's new-fangled ideas to cut up the parsnips to look like chips and

---

1. Felicity painted eight more murals at RAF Middle Wallop, one between each window in a WAAF dining hall.

18. "Cook's Mural" snapshot tipped in Felicity's original manuscript of her mural for a small WAAF cooks' rest room (Other Ranks canteen). RAF Middle Wallop, 1942. Top reads "A heap of candied apples, quince and plum and gourd, with jellies soother [*sic*] than the creamy . . ." She noted, "In distemper on distemper. One colour only (brown), figures approximately life size."

19. *Russia.* Mural and its sketch, one of eight pairs depicting costumes from different countries for a WAAF dining hall. Mural painted distemper on distemper, terra cotta lines picked out with colours and white, three feet six inches high. Sketch in graphite from a sketchbook.

fry them—delicious thought! I happened to be Duty Officer that day, and the mountains of rejected parsnip chips that were shot with barely suppressed rage into the swill-bins were enough to make the toughest dietician weep.

Duty Officers had to cope with other, nondietary, situations as well. All Other Ranks had to be in their quarters by 23.59, or if picked up anywhere outside the camp, show a special late pass, which was not always easy to wangle. There was, of course, no question of WAAF Duty Officers actually going into dormitories, except for an occasional stab-check, but with a Duty Airwoman in tow, as witness or assistant, we would "do the rounds," suggesting that it was time for nattering loiterers to be thinking of going to bed.

In the summer months it went further than that, for there was plenty of long grass around the airfield where necking couples could spend pleasant hours communing with each other. Thus, a torch with a good strong beam was another fairly essential bit of WAAF Duty Officers' equipment. Many's the time I have stood, my torch discreetly focused on a pair of RAF boots and WAAF-issue shoes, while the couple reluctantly disengaged each other. You had to nerve yourself to wait while fly buttons were done up (no quick zips then), hats and other vital items retrieved from the long grass, and the frustrated lovers were finally seen to be on their separate ways.

One evening I was Duty Officer with an assistant who was a very beautiful Canadian WAAF cook, as shy and innocent as she was lovely to look at. We had already been into the NAAFI reminding those there that it was almost closing time and walked down the open area between the barrack blocks, me pushing my bike. Here still stood the old-fashioned, peacetime street lamps, though of course, no longer lit. Suddenly I noticed a balloon tied high up on the little crossbar under one of the lamps itself.

"Hey! Corporal! Look at that!" I said. "Wherever did that come from?"

"Dunno, Ma'am. Didn't notice it before," she said. "It's lovely, isn't it?" Balloons, like many other things, were hard to come by, and it looked very pretty in the moonlight.

"Seems a pity to leave it there." We both started speaking at once, then laughed.

"Well, don't let's!" I said. But neither of us was tall enough to get it down.

"I know what," I suggested, propping my bike against the lamppost. "I'll lift you up and you untie it," which, with a bit of giggling we succeeded in doing. The balloon was a good fifteen inches long and perhaps seven or eight inches in diameter, a beautiful pearly white.

"Who's going to have it?" I asked.

"Oh, you have it, Ma'am. You saw it first!"

We said good night and I mounted my bike and rode off. I swept past the Guardroom, my hat on the back of my head, my Union Jack and red flag illuminated, my pearly white sausage of a balloon floating over my shoulder.

"Good night, Ma'am."

"Good night, Sarge! How d'you like my balloon? Don't find one like this every night tied to a lamppost!"

If there was any laughter, I didn't hear it as I sped back towards the WAAF Officers' quarters. I entered to discover a Squadron Leader Flying in a clinch with a WAAF Code and Cypher, Rosie, on the cretonne sofa of our communal sitting room. They uncoupled themselves and greeted me in a reasonably friendly manner.

"Look what I've got!" I said.

"Where on earth did you find that?"

"Tied to one of the camp's lampposts," I answered.

"Funny!" said the Squadron Leader. "Doesn't look like a Met Office Balloon, they're usually round."

"And red," said Rosie.

"Was it hanging up or down?" asked the Squadron Leader.

"Down, I think," I said. "I really didn't notice."

I threw myself onto the other sofa, my hat, gas mask, and the balloon beside me. We chatted casually for a minute or two.

"Hey!" I said, suddenly, "there's something printed on it."

"What's it say?" said the Squadron Leader, still looking amorously into Rosie's eyes.

I squinted at the end where the string was.

"Hold on. Oh, 'for prevention against disease.'"

There was a second's silence, then a burst of raucous laughter. It took a minute for the truth to dawn on me. I felt a blush rising. The Squadron Leader and Rosie threw themselves into each other's arms again and rolled about with mirth.

"Well neither of you realized straight away either," I said, furiously.

"Was it, hanging up . . . or *down?*" gasped the Squadron Leader, still killing himself with laughter.

But I was too angry to be amused. "It's not *funny,*" I said. "I'm going to report it."

"Oh Ash, *Ash!*" they repeated, still convulsed and clutching each other, "*Don't!*" But I stalked out of the room with the "balloon," closing the door—as well as my ears—to the renewed peals of laughter.

Next morning, the offending object wrapped in a bit of newspaper and carefully tied to the back of my bicycle, I rode down to the Squadron Leader Admin's office, still seething. I leaned my bike so briskly against the wall I never heard the pop. When I came to untie the "evidence" a tattered fragment of the white rubber was all that the flattened bit of newspaper held. But I couldn't turn back now. I had made an appointment to see him. So clutching what was left of my proof I knocked and went in.

"Hullo, Ash. What can we do for you?" he asked cheerfully.

I gave him a smart and formal salute. "Sir!" I said angrily, "I wish to make a complaint."

"Carry on," he said, "I'm listening." Before I was half way through my tale his face had crumpled up with laughter. "Oh, Ash, dear!" he sputtered, holding a handkerchief to his streaming eyes. "What'll I *do* with you? What do you want *me* to do? Have all the pilots of 604 Squadron in here on the mat to tell them they'll be court-marshalled if they blow up any more French letters and tie them to lampposts outside the WAAF quarters? Ash *dear! I ask* you!" He mopped his face again, dissolving into fresh mirth. "Incidentally, is that all the evidence you have left?" I glanced distastefully at the sordid relic in my bit of newspaper, and nodded ruefully.

"Oh *Ash!*" he groaned again.

"But why *should* they get away with it, Sir? It's not *fair!*"

"Life's not fair, Ash. *You* know that! Come on, be a sport! There's a war on! And they're only boys! Let's call it a day! By the way, I thought you'd be coming in about doing a show. Got any ideas yet?"

I screwed up the evidence and threw it angrily into his wastepaper basket. Then I mustered a reluctant smile.

"That's more like it, Ash. Well, have you?"

"Actually, yes. Most of D. Watch at Garlogs are quite keen on doing something."

So the idea of a new show, *Angels Over Base,* got underway, and I would cycle over to Garlogs for rehearsals, pushing the huge, chintz-covered chairs aside in what had been a traditional family drawing room, to give enough space to practice the high kicks for the dance routines. I was developing a line in parodies of popular songs of the moment, to give them a Service slant. There was always a would-be singer (sometimes too ready) to take to the boards as a solo, with or without microphone. The song I chose for a presentable D. Watch singer was Cole Porter's "Miss Otis Regrets," turning her into a corporal.

Corporal Otis regrets, she's unable to dine to-night, Major,
Corporal Otis regrets she's unable to dine tonight.
She told us about your date,
And applied for a pass to stay out extra late, Major,
Corporal Otis regrets she's unable to dine tonight.

On behalf of the WAAF, our CO sends her thanks, Major,
For the way you are trying to help make the girls' lives bright.
For the welcome on your mat,
And the deep divan in your warm and cosy flat, Major,
Corporal Otis regrets she's unable to dine tonight.
We've all learnt a lot from your views on the art of the war, Major,
We know to our cost, all's fair and that Might is Right,
But it seems that you've been doing the rounds,
So we're going to refuse her pass . . . on compassionate grounds,
    Major,
Corporal Otis regrets she's unable to dine tonight.

We also updated several of the sketches that had been used at Fighter Command and Station X, and the show was ready for performance by early that December. It was a big success, and a number of both men and girls from outside the Operations Room asked to take part if I were thinking of doing another, which of course I soon was.

The next show, to be called *Out of the Sun,* was in rehearsal soon after Christmas, and this time I was proud of the fact that the cast of thirty-four included many other trades as well as Clerks S/D. There were cooks, waitresses, MT Drivers, Equipment Assistants, and five RAF Sergeants (quite a catch). Most of these were Fitters and Armourers, who turned out to be extremely useful if we needed real weapons for any of our sketches.

The homemade Victorian melodrama *Shuddering Heights* that we used at Station X was also revived, and the sergeants from the Armoury thoroughly enjoyed their roles as the two international crooks who get out of prison to try and win the hand—and the fortune—of Aspidistra Shudderbottom. We were even asked to do this piece especially at a *Wings for Victory* concert in the Wallop village hall, at which the film star Jessie Matthews was guest artist. Our cast was very bucked up at being photographed with her, though I reckoned she could have played the great film star rather less, and been a bit friendlier and more natural with the troops. But at that date Hollywood stars were still stars.

I was delighted to find that amongst the cooks, who badly needed a boost to their image, there were enough good singers to make a high-class septet! But how to make them *look* glamorous? The poor things were terribly conscious of always smelling of fat because of the hours they stood in front of huge stoves endlessly frying chips, bacon, or sausages and perpetually rendering down fat from all sources for future use.

By a stroke of luck, an old-fashioned haberdashery store in Andover had somehow omitted to reclassify some blue net as being either on Clothing Coupons or "dockets" (the form of rationing that was gradually coming into use for all household goods and materials by the yard). We came back triumphant with bales of the stuff, and made long, slightly bouffant frocks for the seven cooks, in which they almost floated onto the stage to a big round of applause.

20. Felicity's drawing for *Wings* poster. Date unknown. Graphite on paper.

The "Old Growler" Bing Crosby's "I'm Dreaming of a White Christmas" by Irving Berlin was very popular at the moment and asking to be parodied. So we put the smallest of the seven cooks [Jacqueline Cox-Sumner], a marmalade-haired five-footer, into the despised issue WAAF pyjamas, a sort of striped, blue-and-white little-boys flannelette number, and with a spotlight on her she brought the house down singing:

> I'm dreaming of a white nighty,
> Just like the ones I used to wear,
> With its frills and laces,
> In funny places,
> The answer to a Maiden's Prayer.
> I'm dreaming of a white nighty
> Sprinkled with butterflies, and bows,

21. Song for Jacqueline Cox-Summer,
"I'm Dreaming of a White Nighty"
(after Irving Berlin's *White Christmas*).
Performed in *Out of the Sun* at RAF
Middle Wallop, February 1943.

With ribbons and rooshing in rows,
And a little frill to cover up my toes.

I'm dreaming of a white pantie,
Made of the softest crepe-de-chine;
Sprigged with little posies
Of printed roses
And tiddley-bits of ribbon in between;
I'm dreaming [pause] and I'm *still* dreaming!
Tucked in my barrack-bed at night,
May the world soon set itself Right,
And may all my pants and nightdresses be white.

6. The S/O Is Learning

1942–1943

AND WHEN THERE WAS SOME TIME OFF, there was always the Hampshire countryside waiting to be discovered, its empty meadows to be wandered over, its little villages to be cycled through. Broughton was one of these, also mentioned in the Domesday Book, and amongst its attractive little adapted cottages was one called "Grandfathers" whose owners had built their own swimming pool. This was a rarity in the thirties. Mrs. Nita Bompas kindly allowed officers from RAF Middle Wallop to make use of it whenever they liked. She herself patronized and much enjoyed the shows at the camp. As the days lengthened, my roommate and I often cycled over in our free time. I even taught Joyce to dive.

I can't remember exactly when my automatic promotion to Section Officer came through, but it must have been during that autumn or winter. About the same time, *all* WAAF including officers were at last allowed to wear trousers; up until then, only trades like Motor Transport Drivers, Fitters, Balloon Operators, and the like had worn them. True, these desirable garments all opened down the left-hand side, a front opening still being considered an encroachment on the male prerogative and almost indecent (bad luck for the left-handed girls). Even so, this was definitely a plus, especially when bicycling in cold weather. Trousers made me feel one step more emancipated!

Soon after this event, I came into the bar at the Officers Mess one night after a rehearsal to find a group, tankards and glasses in hand, standing round one of the Squadron Leaders Flying. He was a tall, rather old man, the lines of whose face showed a certain harshness, almost bitterness. Few jokes from him did not have a sting in the tail, and his attitude to WAAF officers was less than complimentary.

"So you think it can't be done?" he was saying.

"Well, Sir, if you say so, Sir," a very young pilot put in a little over-boldly.

"You think I can't drink this without touching it with my hands? Right? Want me to show you?"

There was a murmur of assent and the watchers moved in a little closer, myself amongst them. Tilting his head back slightly, the Squadron Leader put his full glass tankard of beer carefully onto his forehead, then moving his hands down, started cautiously undoing the buckle of his belt.

Uh, uh, I thought, here we go! I might have known! But I stayed watching, for in spite of the laughter that greeted this second move, he did not undo his fly, merely wriggled his hips a little so as to make sure his trousers sat more comfortably. Then bit by bit, he lowered himself first into a sitting position on the floor, his head still tilted back so that his forehead with the full tankard on it remained horizontal. Then, drawing in his chin slowly, he started to lie down, ending up stretched out flat on his back.

"Right!" he said, from his prone position. "You still don't believe me, do you? Then watch!"

Slowly he curled himself into a backward summersault, and as his bent legs passed on either side of his ears, his knees clasped behind his back to underline the point, he gripped the edge of the tankard with his teeth and without spilling a drop emptied it down his throat. With sardonic disregard of the applause, he went back to the bar for a refill, which a cluster of young admirers were hurrying to offer him.

I left the bar determined to show him that I could do it just as well as he. I started practicing with a full tin of cocoa (closed) provided by my Catering Officer stable companion, who egged me on. I finally graduated to a tooth mug full of water. The floor of our bedroom was never so well washed as during that period of my efforts. When I'd mastered it, I waited patiently for a suitably casual occasion when the Squadron Leader should be propping up the bar without too big a crowd present.

"Sir! I can do your trick, Sir," I said, edging my way along the bar towards him. He turned his cynical, world-weary gaze upon me.

"Now I wonder which trick would that be, Ash?" he asked.

"The one where you drink your pint without touching it with your hands."

"Ah! So you can do that now, can you, Ash? Well, how about a demonstration?"

"Certainly, Sir."

It was amazing how quickly any little event like that would gather an audience. A ring of interested drinkers quickly assembled as the Squadron Leader offered me a pint. He handed it to me ceremoniously while signalling to the watchers to leave enough space for me to perform properly. I got through it without a hitch, or a drop split, to a round of applause and the Squadron Leader's acknowledgement of a competent rival. The worst part was downing the whole pint of warm beer.

———•———

But there was another world outside the camp with its gossip, its in-jokes and rivalries. The New Year of 1943 showed the tide already turning in the Allies' favour. Before Christmas the Russians had halted the Germans outside Stalingrad.[1] Cinema newsreels showed pictures of the broken and frostbitten remnants of Hitler's Russian Offensive stumbling, disarmed, through snowy wastes to prison camps.

Nowadays people tend to forget that in February of that year Britain presented a Sword of Honour to Stalingrad on the twenty-fifty anniversary of the founding of the Red Army, whose Allies we at the time were. In the same month General Eisenhower took over command in North Africa, Britain began its first heavy raids on European railways and German cities, and the Nazis massacred the Jews in their thousands in Warsaw's burning Ghetto.

Meanwhile, the people of Britain were still supposedly on the alert against a possible Nazi invasion. Posters everywhere went on warning us that "Careless Talk Costs Lives," though Middle Wallop, as I began to realise from my actors in the Armoury, was hilariously ill-equipped to

---

1. Field Marshall Frederich von Paulus led the German Sixth Army against Russia at the Battle of Stalingrad and surrendered it when, weakened by winter and loss of supply lines, his remaining troops faced destruction.

cope with any form of attack from the outside. The nightly patrols round the airfield usually consisted of three airmen with one rifle between them. But this state of affairs was only fully brought home to me in connection with one of the items for our next show.

BBC Radio had recently broadcast a comic adaptation in play form of the famous Gothic thriller *The Mysteries of Udolpho*.[2] I had got the producer's permission to use it, with some alterations, as the pièce de résistance of our next show, *The Stars Look Down*. In one scene we needed a four-poster bed. But how to construct anything that would look like four posts, let alone the attendant curtains? The Armoury Flight Sergeant, now a staunch supporter of all the shows, came up with a suggestion.

"I've got it, Ma'am! Spears."

"What d'you mean, spears?" I asked.

"You know, Ma'am. The spears we have in the Armoury for the parachutists!"

"Parachutists?" I repeated feebly.

Flight turned his eyes heavenward in a gesture of mock despair. "Ma'am, you been on this station for . . . how long is it now, and you haven't realized we've only got one rifle for every three bods?"

"Well, yes," I said dubiously. "But *spears*?"

"Spears, Ma'am. We've got *spears!* Them medi-hee-vial things. *You* know what a spear is! So when all them Nazis come parachuting out of the skies dressed like nuns, you run to us at the Armoury and we issue you with spears, and you *spear* them before they've got time to get out of their harnesses and set up their little fancy radio sets. Got it?"

"Oh, Flight! I don't *believe* it!"

"Want to bet on it? I'll bring some to the next rehearsal."

And he did. Nice newly turned, white-wood broom handles with shining spearheads on the top end. Quite sharp they were, too. We had to be a bit careful with them as they strapped four of them to the legs of an

2. *The Mysteries of Udolpho*, by Ann Radcliff, the eighteenth-century pioneer of the Gothic novel, was also burlesqued by Margaret Nelson Jackson in a radio show titled "Udolpho Revisited" in 1942.

22. Opening chorus for *The Stars Look Down*. Performed at RAF Middle Wallop, May 1943.

ordinary camp bed, then linked them at the top with a canopy-like frill. It hardly ranked with the Great Bed of Ware,[3] but it gave quite a tolerable illusion. "If Hitler only *knew!*" I murmured as we put the finishing touches to the transformation. "Bloody lucky he don't," said the Flight Sergeant with a sniff as he stood back to admire our handiwork. "Udolpho" was the grand finale of the *The Stars Look Down*, which of course, like all its predecessors, was intended primarily to keep everyone laughing.

But I had managed to insinuate into recent shows one serious item which I put just before the interval. This gave the audience a moment of truth about the war before we went on to the next comic act. This time we used the guards' night patrol round the airfield and a failed torch battery as the excuse for reminding our audience of the plight of some of the

3. Now in the British Galleries of the Victoria and Albert Museum in London.

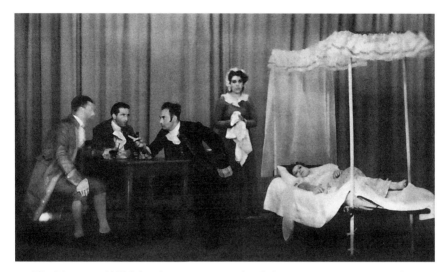

23. *The Mystery of Udolpho.* Armory spears for defense against Nazi parachutists at Middle Wallop used in the play for four-poster bed. Cast *(left to right):* Ferrenzi, Bertolini, Signor Montoni, Caterina, and Emily. "Signor Montoni: 'Let me relate an extraordinary circumstance.'" February 1943.

European countries under Nazi occupation. A Yugoslav, a Greek, a French partisan, and a Russian girl appeared one after another out of the darkness to ask whether Britain still remembered them, or were we "getting soft" now that there were fewer mass raids. The Airman playing the part was a boy from the Armoury who had some time earlier lost a couple of fingers in the course of duty. As he started to defend Britain's record, he stretched out his hand to renew the pledge of support. There was something rather touching about the sight as the partisans placed their ghostly hands on his mutilated one before they faded away again into the darkness to swelling music and the poet [John] Keats's words from his poem "To Autumn," which ends with: "Gone is that vision, do I wake or sleep?"

The Airman came to me afterwards in great excitement and said, "I got them!" He meant of course, the audience, that marvellous moment of stillness when you know that whatever you are saying or doing has got home. "I *had* them . . . in my hand!"

"I know you had," I said. "I felt it too."

Another popular number then was called "My Devotion." The sheet music featured Eric Winstone and his band. As there was always rumbling discontent amongst Other Ranks whose promotion to an extra stripe, or into Commissioned rank, was slow in coming through, I chose that song to parody as a solo.

My promotion,
Is distant and dim as the ocean.
I never thought I should be so long
An ACW 2.
My relations
With other ranks cause complications,
For being used to a Social Sphere
That's well-bred through and through.
I don't know what to do.

Sergeants I have flirted with,
Adjutants I've kissed,
Even shots at Scrambled Eggs
Somehow seem to have missed!

My Commission
Is held up by someone's omission.
I never thought it would take so long
Before my papers came through;
My petitions
Don't alter existing conditions.
Questions were asked in the House, but
There's not much hope in view.
I'm still ACW 2.

Kit Inspection of course was one of the best subjects for mockery in sketches. We did ordinary ones, South Seas Island ones, and Nazi ones. Another variant was the idea of doing a WAAF coming to exchange her knickers at the Equipment Store, in four different musical styles.

Producing the worn-out garment was the only way of getting a replacement, and the fact that for so long all Equipment Assistants had

"Kit Inspections"

"As it would be in Germany"....

"As it would be in the South Seas"....

24. Two scenes from "Kit Inspections."

been men had been a source of great embarrassment to the more sensitive WAAF. Frayed and worn-out detachable collars or the cuffs of shirts were one thing, even stockings with huge holes or discoloured and worn-out feet were possible to exchange without too many blushes. But knickers! That was different. The most shaming things could happen to knickers, which led the shyer WAAF to try and get rid of them rather than bring them back for examination and exchange by a male Equipment Assistant. But their illicit disposal led to all sort of unforeseen complications, not excluding being put on a charge.

But, I thought, turned into a musical item, the theme would be good for quite a few laughs. I chose first the folk song about springtime, the

WAAF coming in holding her pair of disintegrating "blackouts." "It is Exchange Parade I see," she sang,

> With a Hey and a Ho and a Hey, Nonny No,
> With a Hey Nonny Nonny No
> So will you change my pants for me,
> I've worn them, and torn them,
> I mourn them,
> But cannot even pawn them,
> They've had their day, Hey Dinga Linga Ley.
> Hey Dinga Linga Ley,
> Please Corp' don't say me Nay!

It goes on for some time, with a bit of folk dancing to embellish it. Then came Mozart's *Non so piu*, which probably only a fraction of the audience recognized.

WAAF:	If this Clothing Parade's for Exchanging
	I have brought you my panties for changing,
	For the legs are rather frayed at the bottom,
	And the seat is very tattered and torn
	And they're too rotten
	Any girl to adorn,
	Yes too rotten,
	Any girl to adorn.
EQUIP ASST:	Bring them here, let me see their condition,
	Of deceit there must be no suspicion!
WAAF:	Corporal, believe me!
EQUIP ASST:	You could never deceive me!
	I must witness,
	You have split this little knicker in two.

And so on. I wanted to end up in Grand Opera style with Wagner, so I put in the modern one as Number 3, based on a popular song by Jerome Kern and Oscar Hammerstein II: *All the Things You Are.*

| WAAF: | These are the promised pair of knickers, |
| | That make the Wallop winter seem warm. |

EQUIP ASST: They are the answer to your prayer,
              Though not designed to flatter the female form.

The finale was the "Pilgrims' Chorus" from *Tannhauser* and though again, not many of the audience recognized it, it had them in fits, for the WAAF, now well padded out as a proper Wagnerian heroine, came on with her tattered knickers impaled on one of the Armoury spears.

> Is this parade
> For the exchanging of clothing?
> My pants are frayed,
> And I regard them now with loathing,
> They can no more adorn
> Me, for they are all torn,
> I trust their condemnation won't be too long delayed!

At the end, both WAAF and Equipment Assistant still singing at the tops of their voices went offstage, completely drowned by the few brass instruments we had been able to muster as accompaniment.

———•———

It was about then that the American presence really began to be felt in that part of Britain. WAAF Admin Officers were given special guidelines as to how to explain the difference between the Yanks and our own boys. The language was nominally the same, but the use of words was so different. The British girl, though heaven knows by no means always a shy violet, often completely misunderstood the approach of the American, whether black or white, when he used the fulsome phraseology that was taken for granted back home.

"Gee, Honey! You look like a million dollars tonight," meant no more in real terms than the Brit's mumbled, "You look like a bit of all right!"

But even more compelling than the unintended flattery in the words were the rolls of banknotes that could be seen sticking out of the hip pockets of the average GI. And not only did they have much more pay, but their PX stores were equipped with things we hadn't seen for years. Our poor Airmen soon found they were losing out in the popularity stakes, with no bars of chocolate to produce at the cinema or pairs of silk stockings to slip into a pocket with a good-night kiss.

25. Mock circus cast from *The Show Goes On.* "The complete team."

A last but by no means insignificant detail was the difference in the cut of the trousers. The RAF Other Ranks "issue" was of a roughish, slightly hairy cloth, made to be worn with braces, and often hitched up almost to the armpits. The Yanks, *per contra,* used a material of a quality nearly indistinguishable from our officers' uniform cloth, cut apparently by tradition for wear with a belt, or even to fit snugly round the hips without any visible means of support. Thus they somehow looked more confident, of a better class, and our girls in uniform, starved as they were of all frills, could be forgiven for succumbing to the chaps who had a bit extra to offer.

But change of yet another kind was in the air, and by about October it was common knowledge that Middle Wallop itself was soon to be handed over to the Americans. We got in one more show before the target date, somewhat ironically called *The Show Goes On,* and for the grand finale we ambitiously staged a mock circus. For this we hired a pantomime horse from the theatrical costumier Fox in London. But I had got somewhat bored with the traditional opera choruses and thought we must do something different for this, the station's very last show. After much consultation with the cast, we decided that our Armoury Flight Sergeant, now quite a practiced performer, should be a modern Mark Antony addressing the funeral crowd at Middle Wallop's demise.

26. *The Show Goes On.* "The Strong-Men: Monsewer and May-dam Trumble (Premier High-Diving Team of America) and two Fairies."

So, partially clothed in male issue underwear with a bit of mock tiger skin over the vital parts—his costume for the circus finale—he strode onto the stage and took the audience by surprise declaiming:

Airwomen! Airmen! And Officers! Lend me your ears!
We come to bury gloom and not to praise it.
The good jokes that we make live after us,
The bad ones go to swell the Salvage Drive.
So let it be in Wallop! Yet I'm miserable!
(to the stage crowd) You're miserable!
(to the audience) We're *all* miserable!
And *why?* Because our Show has got no Opening!
You blocks, you stones, you worse than senseless things!
Know you not Korda? Cecil B. de Mille?
You puny, service-impregnated minds
Can think of nothing!
Days and weeks, nay years
The Intellectuals of Middle Wallop
Have wracked their softened brains in vain endeavour
To find an Opening that is *different!*

Something with glamour! Something that's divine!
Even Air Ministry can think of nothing!
Nothing! Not even through "the usual channels."
So we must needs content ourselves with hoping
The Show can still go on *without* an opening!
Shall we begin?

The stage crowd shouts "Yes!" and to a roll of drums, disappears, leaving the Flight Sergeant alone in a heroic pose, at which point the circus horse appears, having mistaken the beginning for the end. The Flight, who was a popular figure, mounts him (with a bit of difficulty in spite of rehearsal). The show proper then starts with very encouraging applause.

It was in the confusion accompanying the winding up of the station, which followed soon after this event, that the horse was temporarily mislaid. This was odd, since you'd have thought it could hardly have fitted into any RAF Inventory category, not even "Horse, circus, Entertainment Officer, for the use of," without being noticed. An unintelligible telegram which created a lot of mirth as it was passed from officer to officer did nothing to clarify matters. It read: "Return Horse Immediately Stop Fox." Eventually somebody said, "What about asking Ash? Maybe it's got something to do with her last show?" A dejected creature was retrieved just in time from a heap of unidentifiable "salvage" and hurriedly dispatched.

It was during the autumn I found to my great surprise that I had been mentioned [commended] in Dispatches. There was no heroism involved, nor was it because I was "somebody's Popsy," as one of my officer colleagues, to my rage, suggested. I think it was just that the Station Commander, Group Captain Stephen Hardy, noticed and appreciated a hard worker. He must just have liked the way I got on with things. He was a very tall and rather sad man, cutting an almost de Gaulle-like figure, just too young to have taken an active, flying part in World War I, and by the time it came to World War II, just too old. I was told that he had found it hard to reconcile himself to having "missed it" again, and to not being allowed to put theory into practice by himself knocking some German pilots out of the skies. He was another of the orthodox Regulars who never pulled me up about my undone top button, nor the defiant angle of my cap.

I don't remember much about the actual wind-down of the Station before the handing-over date, though there did seem to be an atmosphere of "drink and be merry for tomorrow the Yanks'll be here!" One evening the Armoury Officer, usually a peaceable and sober enough type, got so drunk he went round shooting up all the ceiling lights in the Mess. It was quite a job to disarm him before he was tempted by other targets.

But gradually numbers thinned, with the Orderly Room working itself into a state of frenzy as both RAF and WAAF, Other Ranks and Officers, were individually posted away. At the very last moment it was decided to throw a party for all officers' wives and other locals who had been connected with the station over the years.

"Why let the Yanks have any of our booze allocation? Might as well drink the lot up!" was the sentiment behind it. And did the "civilians" get drunk! Especially the women. I was quite shocked, for I had not realized to what an extent those of us in uniform had learnt how to carry our drink.

Leaving Middle Wallop was sadder for me than leaving any previous station, or as it turned out, any subsequent one. I had grown more self-confident and made more friends there than I had so far made anywhere else. And I had had great fun.

Among the new friends I had spent quite a lot of time with was one of the Medical Officers, a Scot who hoped after the war to become a composer. He was particularly interesting in the Lallans Scot poets and, in general, in setting poems to music. Since my sister Mary had been a singer before marriage and the making of a family, it was the branch of music that interested me most. John also introduced me to a new world of psychological ideas which we spent hours discussing. The only problem was where to find a secluded spot in which to have such lovely intellectual arguments.

John was interested in my drama activities too, for we had compared notes on the fact that one "problem WAAF," whom he knew about because of her tendency to kleptomania, never slipped up during periods of rehearsal before a show. Apparently, if she had enough of the limelight, there was no urge driving her to be light-fingered.

On one occasion, coming back from a long walk, we were caught in a storm and took refuge, crouching in the outhouse of the nearest Married Quarters which we reached just in time. We *had* to finish what we were talking about. If we had gone into the Mess it would have been cut short by the inevitability of calling "shop." We carried on regardless, as the thunder rolled and the rain beat down on the corrugated iron out-house roof. If anyone saw us emerging afterwards, it would merely have confirmed the assumptions being made about us, which I of course was totally unaware of at the time. I knew he had an attractive and pregnant young wife, herself part-qualified as a doctor as well. And anyway, as far as I was concerned at least, it was a genuine "meeting of minds," though everyone apparently assumed we were otherwise employed.

It was with John that I explored the mysterious, ancient hump of Danebury Hillfort, still unexcavated, guarding its secret.

> Danebury, like a Chinese drawing
> Ringed by a foggy shroud,
> With the misty fingers of many searchlights
> Fumbling the tufted cloud.
> And when the thunder rumbles away,
> And the sky's washed clear of rain,
> Orion winks at the small red beacons,
> Winking back again.[4]

I had no idea where I was going to land up next for I was suddenly posted to a so-called Refresher Course in, of all extraordinarily lucky places, Windermere in the Lake District.

---

4. Also published in *Time and Tide,* 1944.

7. Via Windermere to "Y"

1943–1944

IT WAS REALLY RATHER SURPRISING that the RAF should have requisitioned what must, after all, have been a hotel of some standing in a beauty spot such as Lake Windermere for the unlikely purpose of a series of WAAF Officer Refresher Courses. It was certainly a stroke of luck for us who found ourselves posted there for a whole month.

The Bowness Hotel was in a unique position on the lake and I, who had never been to the Lake District before, at once fell under the spell of its autumn beauty, Keats's "Season of mists and mellow fruitfulness" if ever there was one.[1] As I was between postings, I had all my goods and chattels with me, including my bicycle. Truanting from some of the lectures was not at all difficult.

Most of them were pretty basic, and boring. In the Hygiene Field the four years of war did not seem to have broken much new ground. Intercourse between bees and flowers, rather than between humans, and whether VD could be caught from lavatory seats and cracked cups, were still current topics. So I turned to the pages on Buggery and Sodomy in the copies of the Manual of Air Force Law thoughtfully provided for us, and they proved decidedly more interesting and informative.

I found a kindred spirit in Betty, a WAAF Officer I knew, and we managed to hire a bike for her, though finding one's way around with no maps and no signposts did not make for rapid navigation. But the Lakes are a beautiful as well as a healthy place to take time off in, whether on two legs or two wheels, for there are as many hills to be walked up as there are to be sometimes dangerously cycled down. Betty and I found one truly

---

1. Ashbee quotes John Keats, from his poem *To Autumn* (1819).

magical experience. On a twenty-four hours off, we cycled and pushed our bikes miles up into unknown fell territory before mist began to close in on us.

We did not know, since we had not met a living soul to ask, that we had reached Brothers Water. In the now swirling whiteness we stumbled upon what looked as if it might be a tiny inn. There was no bell and no reply to our knocking so we pushed the door and it opened. We found ourselves in a warm, low-ceilinged room with half a dozen shining black oak tables on each of which was a little bowl of fresh, glowing, red and purple anemones.

We looked at each other unbelievingly, laughing to see the fog like hoarfrost on our hair and eyelashes, and marvelling at what seemed a step backwards into a vanished age of grace. When a woman appeared and actually asked us if we wanted scones with our tea, we were bewitched. And they even had a room free so that we could stay the night. We had supper by candlelight, and bacon and eggs for breakfast the next morning. The memory is as sharp and clear as if it were yesterday.

At the end of the four weeks I was posted to RAF Newbold Revel, in Warwickshire, another county new to me. In spite of my "unreliable" past record, I seemed to be destined for postings to stations with mysterious coded letters in addition to their names. Bletchley Park had answered to code name "X", Newbold Revel was "Y", and apparently equally secret.

Volume 6, "Warwick," in L. F. Salzman's *Victoria History of the Counties of England* gives no indication that the RAF requisitioned the house during the war.[2] Perhaps it was too secret a transaction for even the scholars of so respectable a publication to have been allowed information. At the date of that volume's appearance (1951) it would have been covered by the 30 Year Rule.[3] This volume merely says that the house was bought in 1931 by the

2. Ashbee does not identify the building, though Newbold Revel was a manor house near Rugby in Warwickshire. RAF Newbold Revel began life in late 1942 as 367 Wireless Unit. Ashbee probably refers to L. F. Salzman's *Victoria History of the County of Warwick*, vol. 6 (1951).

3. The 30 Year Rule specified that official records be made public through the National Archives only after that time had passed. In 1968 this rule replaced the 50 Year Rule that

British Advent Missions Ltd. of Watford and in 1946 was acquired by the Sisters of Charity of St. Paul as a Training College for Teachers.

I hope by then someone had tackled the rat holes in the skirting boards of all of the bedrooms. They were so large that it was difficult to find enough scarce newspaper to stuff them. We had been told that the previous owners had been Seventh-day Adventists who wouldn't kill anything, hence the rats.

It was the first time I had actually had a room to myself, so instead of trying to disregard a restless or possibly snoring sleeper in a neighbouring bed, my ear was nervously tuned to any sign that a surviving rat might be working its way through the screwed up wodges of *Daily Mirror, Herald,* or *Morning Post* to return to its previous hunting ground. No amount of RAF fumigation had been able to dispose of the giant cockroaches, either. They continued to roam the spacious Victorian kitchens, circumnavigating the vast black cast-iron ranges. When we came in for late cups of watery cocoa at night, we would see the cockroaches scurrying for cover, clattering like miniature tanks over the stone-flagged floors.

By 1943, anyway, "Y" had something to do with the war against Japan, and the material was so secret that it could not be flown over to America for officers to be trained there. Officers had to be flown to Britain to be "indoctrinated" at Newbold Revel. Everything for this training was housed in some outlying huts to which no one except the special instructors and their pupils, Yank visitors or others, were allowed to approach. We were asked to be especially nice to this first batch of about a dozen Americans, whose names alone were a sort of roll-call of the New World: Fernicola, Warren, Gonzales, Schmidt, Loeb, Spears, and so on.

Concealing, we hoped politely, any hint of superiority, we gave them a rundown on the course of the war. We were secretly delighted when several of them, on a day off in London, were caught in an air raid and were herded into one of the makeshift shelters of London's Underground stations for a taste (and smell!) of "true British grit" in action. These air

---

had previously been in effect. The 30 Year Rule was made redundant when the Freedom of Information Act went into effect in 2005.

raids on London in the middle of February 1944 were the heaviest the city had been subjected to since May 1941.

Our New Yorker, Loeb, who had asked my advice as to how he could find himself "a little bit of fluff" while in London, was one of those thus initiated. The bit of fluff he had picked up had obviously been in no mood for heroism, dollars or no dollars, and had ensured that he dived down with her into the deepest shelter near her pad. When we heard his excited description of his adventures, a few looks passed surreptitiously among us veterans.

One of the Yanks, called Charlie, rather thought he fancied me, so I decided the best thing to do for his "education" would be to find him a bike and cycle with him over to Coventry to see the devastation wrought on the city by the Blitz. Wandering through the shattered city centre and looking up at the blackened, jagged remnant of the pinkish tower of the Cathedral had a powerful effect on him for which I liked him the better.

Camp life at Newbold Revel was not exactly scintillating. There was no camp as such to cycle round, nor remote WAAF hostels to visit in the course of duty, and after Middle Wallop I felt limited and restricted. Nor did I really take to either of the other WAAF officers I had to work with. It was a case of grinning and bearing it, and seeking out what there was to hand.

We did have on the station a remarkable Sergeant Cook, name of Mould. He was short and neat with a round head of pitch-black hair, the immaculate lacquer of which we learned with fascination was achieved by an application of cooking lard. No new-fangled Brilliantine for Sergeant Mould. Before being called up he had run a Fish 'n' Chips shop somewhere in the East End of London, and his dream after the war was to have a chain of a dozen such enterprises. But he had another passion on the side, and that was ballroom dancing.

Appalled at the behaviour and sloppy carriage of the average erk, he decided that ballroom dancing classes were what they needed, and he proceeded to organize them and instruct in them himself. Dancing had never been my strong suit. Given the choice, or chance, I had always preferred shinning up a rope or throwing myself over a high jump, or from a diving board. And because I had been quite tall from the age of about thirteen, I had always had to dance "man" in the dancing classes I had been forced to attend as part of the education of a "young lady." This was no help when I was later faced with being pushed around a dance floor by someone of the opposite sex who needed a partner able to follow him in his attempts at performing the tango or foxtrot.

It turned out that Charlie was an enthusiastic dancer, and when he heard of Sergeant Mould's initiative, he suggested we support it. Somewhat reluctantly, I agreed, and we presented ourselves at the next hop. The gormless erks stood round the sides of the room, still too shy to risk trying out their new skill, while the WAAF danced with each other. Suddenly Charlie dragged me onto the floor with him, and Sergeant Mould, seeing his chance, followed suit by grabbing any uncoupled WAAF and erk, welding their reluctant hands together, and propelling them onto the dance floor to join Charlie and me. All were soon gyrating to that most popular number at the time, Irving Berlin's "Cheek to Cheek."

But my feet in their WAAF-issue shoes were not up to it, and in no time I had been tripped up by Charlie's nimble footwork and was thrown into his arms, my cheek suitably pressed against his. To my deep embarrassment he took this as a sign of my growing affection and pressed his advantage, and when my next forty-eight hours off came up, Charlie wanted to come with me.

But as I was to visit my sister Mary in Marlborough, very pregnant with her number-two child and coping in unsympathetic lodgings with the not yet three-year-old first one, I didn't think that would be a very good idea. Mary was camp-following her husband, Ted, now a Radar Operator at nearby Yatesbury. I did agree, though, that Charlie might accompany me as far as London if he liked. In the train I had a bright idea.

"How would you like to meet a friend of mine?" I suggested. "She's very nice, answers to the name of Pyddy. We joined up together. Only she got out again while you still could, felt she could be more useful outside. She works at the Ministry of Information now. If you play your cards right, she might even show you around. Shall I give you her number?" Rather unwillingly Charlie agreed.

As I had to change trains at Reading, I thought I'd give Pyddy a ring just to tell her a Yank friend of mine might be getting in touch. I got through quite quickly in spite of an initial tussle with buttons A and B.

"Hi! Pyddy," I said, "Just a quick one to say . . ."

"I know!" she laughed. "He's been on to me already!"

"Didn't waste much time," I said, mildly surprised. "But he's very nice. You'll like him."

A prophetic statement as it turned out. They were engaged within a fortnight. And it has proved a very successful union, though they did not succeed in actually getting married until after the end of the war. So many GIs concealed the fact that they had left a wife behind in the States, sometimes even marrying bigamously, that a very strict system of checks had to be initiated before a Yank and a British girl were actually allowed to get to the altar together. Charlie was posted to Japan before all the paperwork came through, and Pyddy had to risk going over to the States on her own, to be ready for his return from the Far East once the war ended.

And then I was suddenly sent to preside over a Court of Enquiry on a remote Radar Station in North Wales where the Station Commander had been "fancying around" with his WAAF. Someone had spilt the beans by reporting on him. It was, I believe, a perfectly normal Court of Enquiry according to the rules laid down in the *Manual of Air Force Law,* but I found it surprising, to say the least. I was supposed to conduct such semilegal proceedings, take evidence from all concerned, and finally make some kind of judgment followed by a report. Very fortunately for me, although I was officially in charge, a pleasant and sensitive RAF Officer in the education part of the Service, together with another with experience of the law—he was there to ensure that legal niceties were observed—arrived at the same time to help me through this distinctly alarming ordeal.

The Station Commander on the mat was a good looking young man, and I imagine that the isolation of the place—a beautiful, desolate spot with wild seas breaking over rocky coves, and seagulls mournfully calling—coupled with the forced proximity of a number of sometimes very attractive young women, had just been too much for his standards of morality.

We three "judges" had our meals brought up to us in the seclusion of the rooms put at our disposal while "the accused" had his, under guard, somewhere else. It was sometimes difficult to keep a straight face while taking evidence from the WAAF, who had to describe what their Station

Commander had been getting up to, while at the same time avoiding giving the impression that they were "ladies of easy virtue."

But when I got back again to Newbold Revel, I found that my Admin
duties on the station did not use me up any more than they had done
before, or on other stations with far more to offer than Newbold Revel.
And I missed the camaraderie of Middle Wallop terribly. What could I do
except start planning another show?

We called this one *New and Bold,* and again the material was all our
own, though of course it was possible to dish up some of the sketches used
before. The "Kit Inspections" turn had been developed to include a full-
blown Nazi version, as well as a South Sea Island one. In this version the
WAAF had to account for the right complement of grass skirts, bracelets,
and anklets. Their "issue" bras decorated with raffia and artificial flowers
went down very well (see p. 89).

We also had at the time a station Padre who was a great character.
He had a walleye—it might even have been a glass one—and was minus
a couple of fingers on one hand. He claimed his greatest triumph in the
pulpit had been when he once inadvertently gave a successful racing tip
for the 3.30. It had taken him some time after that to understand why his
congregations had so miraculously increased.

I never heard him preach, as I steadfastly refused to go to church.
On the occasions when I had to take the Church Parade, I would do all
the assembling, wheeling, and marching of my flock, and then let them
file into the actual building without me. This was permitted in King's
Regulations, to allow for the odd "infidel" who might have reached officer rank. With me it was a point of principle, though it was often colder
hanging about outside, since I had to be ready to get all my flock lined up
again on coming out of the service to be marched back to their barracks
for Sunday dinner.

The Padre, who took my education in hand as regards playing bil-
liards, was game to play any role in the show, though he had considerable
difficulty in mastering his words. But he made up for it by his blood-
curdling characterization of Sir Willoughby Shudderbottom, the Victorian father of Aspidistra in the melodrama *Shuddering Heights,* which we
revived yet again with its usual success.

27. *Shuddering Heights*. The Padre as Sir Willoughby Shudderbottom. "Ha! Madam. So I have found you!"

But I was restive. The Russians had turned the tide in the Ukraine and were now advancing westwards, clamouring ever more loudly for the Americans and the British to open a Second Front. But although the papers from time to time calculated about this, there seemed as yet small sign of its happening, though the Allies were working their way up Italy and by 1944 were launching their big attack on Monte Cassino.

A boy my family had befriended from childhood, who had joined the Army on the outbreak of war and had survived Dunkirk although he could not swim, was killed on the Anzio beachhead. Jimmy and I had met from time to time to compare notes about our progress in the Forces. He had got his corporal's tapes before I had mine. Then, just as mine came through he was made a sergeant. Then I had overtaken him by getting a commission! Now he was gone, a loved bit of my childhood merely a name on a headstone in an Italian war cemetery.

I was still in touch with Ruth Black-Hawkins, the WAAF Admin Officer who had been my boss at Station X, and who had helped me get my transfer out of Intelligence. I rang her up and poured out my dissatisfaction about Newbold Revel. "Well," her astringent voice and raucous laugh came over the phone, "get a posting. Don't just sit there moaning."

"But how?" I asked.

"Ring Air Ministry."

"But I don't know anyone in High Quarters to ring up! I don't know anyone I could tip a wink to. I'd have to go through the proper channels, and I've no good reason, compassionate or other, to ask, really."

"Oh, come on, Ash. Have a bit of spunk. Just ring up one of the more senior WAAF Officers at Air Ministry. That's what I did. It worked a treat. I'll give you a name. You can think up some plausible story, I'm sure."

I was far from confident, even with the Wing Officer's name she gave me to try. Ruth was a much more self-confident person than I was then, and quite capable of brazening out something irregular. Of course I made a mess of it.

I got the wrong WAAF Officer, couldn't find a plausible way of having a speech with the one whose name I'd been given, and when it was winkled out of me that all I wanted was to get away from Newbold Revel, I was roundly attacked for trying to bypass "the proper channels" and wangle something by irregular means. I was near tears when I put down the phone. Obviously this was a situation I'd never been in before, and I had no idea how seriously my "indiscretion" would be regarded, and whether some black mark would appear on my records somewhere to rebound on me at a later date. As far as I can remember, no letter of accusation followed on to the ticking off I'd had on the phone, and a couple of weeks went by without development of any kind.

Then suddenly my posting came through. I was to report—of all places—to RAF Ottercops Moss, in Northumberland, the old CH (Chain Home) Station twenty-nine miles northwest of Newcastle.[4] Ottercops Moss! The joke station up by the Roman Wall that always got aircraft mixed up with thunderstorms. It was practically off the map, even if it had been the first station to pick up Rudolf Hess that moonlit May night of 1941.

4. For Chain Home, refer to chapter 3, p. 45n3.

If proof were needed that I was in disgrace, this was it. I had tried to pull strings and failed. There was nothing for it now but to get my things together, make my good-byes and report as the signal instructed, to the Back of Beyond!

PART 3

From the Sticks to the Cradle

February 1944–July 1946

8. The Glint of Roman Spears

1944

TRAVELLING BY TRAIN was a slow process during the war years. Even if it were not a question of an air raid happening, or of the lines having been disrupted by a recent attack, troop trains or trains carrying vital supplies usually took precedence. Ordinary passenger coaches could sit for lengthy periods just waiting for a go-ahead signal. It was difficult to know where you were, too, for all station names had been removed as a means of confusing the expected German parachutists.

First-time travellers were additionally nonplussed (as assuredly logical German invaders would also have been) by the number of stations apparently called VIROL or OXO or BOVRIL, for the huge enamelled ads for these products (VIROL was yellow letters on a dark-blue ground) had nothing but the single word to tell you that they were a tonic or a soup additive or a nourishing drink. You might have had a clue if you had seen the famous ad which had a man in his pyjamas riding a rough sea, his arms and legs curled round the familiar squat brown glass jar underneath which were the words "BOVRIL prevents that sinking feeling."

But if the journey stretched into the hours of darkness, the train's blackout blinds would be drawn down, and in a light too dim to read by, the crowded, usually smoke-filled carriage would become a friendly substitute for club, or pub, or even air-raid shelter, with everyone talking to everyone else, sharing their bomb experiences or their anxieties about loved ones serving overseas.

Warwick to Newcastle, the nearest station to Ottercops, was such a journey, though I can't remember how long it took nor how I actually got to the RAF station itself. Probably, as I was an official posting and because I had all my possessions and, of course, my bicycle with me, the station van may have been deputed to meet me. The normal method of getting to and from the camp turned out to be a battered bus, run by a local family of near bandits with an almost total disregard for the safety of the passengers. As the road led out of the blackened squalor of Newcastle itself, you could feel the years of industrial history gradually dropping away until only the great, treeless, lonely fells were left with their tiny ridges of drystone walls crisscrossing the emptiness.

And the sheep! Sheep and emptiness.

The reason for the existence of the station was its Chain Home transmitter, though of course all these radar stations always had two: the great, metal, two-platformed transmitting tower, and the smaller though still quite high wooden receiving one. Early technology had required that they be sited on the highest point of the locality, so the transmitter, like a giant piece of Meccano, dominated the hill above Otterburn, clouds sailing past it on blowy days and at other times apparently beheaded by swirling mists.

It was the same Otterburn, I soon realised, made famous in the old ballads about the Northumberland Percys, and the Scots Douglases who met them in gory combat at the Battle of Otterburn in 1388.

When Percy with the Douglas met,
    I wat he was fu' fain
They swakkit swords till sair they swat
    Till the bluid ran down like rain. . . .

There are three versions of this great contest, a Scottish and an English one, both called "The Battle of Otterburn," and a second English one, "Chevy Chase." The Scots one is the more poetic, but all agree on one thing: it was a very bloody battle, with statistics of slaughtered Scottish and English knights varying according to which version you chose to read.

Ottercops Moss's days as a significant part of Britain's defences were numbered. This was mainly because the newer, more sophisticated radar equipment, capable of much greater accuracy and also of detecting lower-flying incoming aircraft, had by degrees been installed all along the East Coast of Britain. It was also the natural result of the progress of the war itself. So there were only three officers on the station beside myself.

The Station Commander, a Flight Lieutenant, had obviously been posted to "the sticks" to get him out of the way without forcibly retiring him. On my arrival he informed me that he had a metal plate in his head as a result of a World War I wound, and that this had partially paralyzed his right hand. He proved the point by shaking hands with me, a slightly daunting proceeding as I found I had to use my other hand to detach myself from his cold and nerveless grip.

His only claim to fame appeared to be that his wife had been the mistress of Hannan Swaffer, the well-known journalist and drama critic. Perhaps it was this vicarious contact with the naughty world of the stage that gave him value, but it was a trifle difficult to know how to react the first time. Did one say, "Congratulations, Sir," or "Jolly good show?" But I soon got used to it, as he would tell his story to any new listener before he was onto his second treble whisky.

The other officers were a sleazily joking Engineer Officer, with the rank of F/O (Flying Officer), and a midget Welsh Admin Officer, recently commissioned. The little Welshman A/F/O (Assistant Flying Officer) had been, until called up, a village post office official, so for him translation to this rural spot did not present any great challenge.

Had I been a blonde bombshell, the F/O Engineer would doubtless have made a pass at me, but I was not his type and in any case I was in such a state of depression at my "banishment" that I would not have been susceptible to any blandishments.

A third, very young Technical Officer turned up not long after my arrival but he was almost straight from school or polytechnic and, though very sweet and gentle, was still a bit wet behind the ears. He was the first person I had ever met who said he had not been able to do his school homework without having the wireless on. To my family, who first moved into the gramophone world in the early 1930s, and had acquired a radio only shortly before the outbreak of war, the idea that music could be an unlistened-to background accompaniment was extraordinary.

What was I going to do with myself and these uninspiring companions, especially during the evenings? Then it turned out that the midget Welshman could at least play chess. "If there was a set," he added.

"I have one," I said, and fetched the tiny three-inch-square portable that my Yank admirer Charlie had given me.

"That's a nice little job," said the Welshman. "Where d'you get that from?"

"A Yank friend of mine found it in the desert," I replied. "North African campaign. Left behind by some dead chap in a tank."

In spite of the practice I had had with my lesbian bedfellow in the early days of the war, I was never more than a defensive player. I could only see a couple of moves ahead and had never got as far as studying "opening gambits" or "end-games." Suddenly the little Welshman would look startled, and leaning over the tiny set with a puzzled expression, he would say, "Now what have you got up your sleeve this time?" He would then glance up at me suspiciously.

I would look down with, I hoped, concealed surprise. My thoughts had wandered while waiting for his move and there was of course nothing up my sleeve at all. But I summoned up an enigmatic smile and said, "Aha!" This would preface another long pause, while he tried to work out what sinister move I was considering. But he usually won, which gave him enormous satisfaction, for he was otherwise quite unable to sum me up. He was, to say the least of it, uneasy in my company, especially after one episode when we were doing the rounds of the camp together. Usually I did this alone.

Coming out into the sparkling spring air, I stood for a moment and just looked around me. On every side the fells rolled in curves, still in their winter colouring, an almost greyish green, no hedges, just the low dry-stone walls subdividing them into unevenly shaped fields. An occasional isolated clump of trees, sometimes nestling in a hollow, sometimes dark against the sky, would be the only other feature.

And everywhere the sheep.

No one, it seemed to me, had made any mark on this land since the Romans. Not even all those battling Northumbrian Lords, Earls, and Knights in the train of the Percys, nor the Scottish nobles who in their hundreds had raided the district, cattle-rustling and provoking the Percys to fight back.

If you turned left out of the camp, though, and took the road down to Otterburn itself, where the Percy Arms still stood, a beautiful, old, weathered grey stone building, full of history, you could feel them closer there. But not looking out from the camp; from there it was still only the Romans.

Not on too clear a day,
Nor in the transient light of windy weather,
When shadow-clouds
Chase one another over blackened heather.
A little haze, and the thin distant cry
Of April lambs, black-faced with velvet ears,
And I,
Watching the empty skyline of the fell
For pointed Roman spears.

Here is no time. A thousand, thousand sheep
Have rubbed their fleeces on the grey stone walls,
Present and past are one.
A cuckoo calls;
Kingcups and eagle standards, both are gold;
Rumble of chariot wheels, or distant drone
Of a belated bomber limping home.
A small wind stirs; the evening air grows cold.
That vanished glint of sun . . .
Was it the helmets and the kilts of Rome?

The weekly magazine *Time and Tide* actually published that poem of mine in 1945, but by then I was long gone from Ottercops Moss, and my little Welshman never knew about it. If he had, it would have confirmed his worst suspicions about my sanity.

For on one of those days when he and I were going the rounds together, we paused at the exact spot where I always stopped to look over the fells. It was a bright day, and I shaded my eyes with my hand as I stared at the horizon.

"What are you looking at?" he asked.

"Can't you see them?" I said, my eyes still fixed on the distance. "See what?" he said, trying to follow my gaze.

I turned to look at him, as though in disbelief. "You mean . . . you really can't see them?"

"See *what?*" Now he was getting worried.

I laid my hand gently on his arm and felt him almost shrink from my touch. "That glint of gold!" I said softly, "just coming over the horizon . . . on the rim of the hill . . . the glint of Roman spears!" It was a bit wicked of me, I know. Poor chap. He never felt comfortable when left in a room alone with me after that.

One day the F/O Engineering said he'd got to check something to do with the maintenance. "Want to climb one of the towers?" he asked.

"Oh yes, please."

"You don't mind the heights?" he said, looking at me condescendingly. "They're higher than you think."

And they were, or rather, it was; for in fact, he only suggested when it came to it that I go up the receiving tower. This was the wooden one, about two-thirds the height of the transmitting tower. It looked rather like those slightly primitive derricks I'd seen pictures of in books about the Baku oil fields in the south of the Soviet Union. Even so, I had to wear a cumbrous safety harness, the large hook of which had to be clamped each time onto the rung of the ladder, two above the one I was climbing onto.

Presumably it was just an extra safety regulation (I noticed the F/O Engineer was wearing one too) for our progress was not actually up the outside of the tower's structure, where every gust from the North Sea or the Roman Wall could have swept one to oblivion. The higher we climbed, the more the structure swayed, and though wild horses would not have dragged the admission from me, I was quite glad when we reached the top that we were on the somehow slightly cosier wooden tower and not even higher, on the lacy Meccano of the transmitter.

I was frequently trying to find the Station Commander to sign some letters or put his mark to some file that I had dealt with when he had not been able to be found. We had a tough old RAF Flight Sergeant in the Orderly Room who had no illusions about the CO at all, though he was loyal enough not to say in so many words that he was "drunk and incapable."

"Seen the CO anywhere this morning, Flight?" I would ask, putting my head round the Orderly Room door.

"Not in the Officers' Mess, Ma'am?" he would inquire, not looking up from his preparation of Standing Orders.

"Not a sign."

"Tried the Sergeants' Mess, Ma'am? He drops in there sometimes for the odd, er . . . well, just to see how the chaps are getting on."

"Hadn't thought of looking in there," I said the first time it happened.

"Failing that, take a decko in the Airmens' Mess. He sometimes drops in there."

"Thanks, I'll try the Sergeants' Mess first." And there I found him, sound asleep in a battered club chair, with a half-drunk glass of neat whisky beside him. I woke him up and offered him the letters to sign; he barely glanced at them. "Good girl, Ash, you've got it all in hand, I'm sure." As I walked back to my own office it struck me that one of my tasks might well be to check the station's booze allocation to see if we really *needed* all that whisky.

As I was the Catering Officer as well as the WAAF Admin I found I was more or less in charge of the ordering of stores, including the booze allocation for the Officers' Mess. There was some kind of an RAF Depot at Rothbury, and we would sometimes have to drive over in the station van to collect special items. The bank was in Hexham, another drive through the empty fells. Money was collected from there, also put in the van, before the weekly Pay Parades. When I came to look at the Officers' Mess booze allocation seriously, it seemed an enormous quantity for the few of us still left there and obviously dated from the time when the station strength had been much greater.

So I cut it by half. When the CO found out, he was spluttering with rage. "But Sir," I said. "There are only five of us. We don't need all that booze. Specially not all those bottles of whisky. There's still plenty for your nightcap. Anyway, doesn't it look to you as though Air Ministry is really going to close us down soon? Shall I ring up and check if there's a date yet?" But he had stumped off in a fury. I decided to try on my own.

It took a long time to get London, and even longer to find anyone who knew anything about our neck of the woods. At last a faint female voice said, "Sorry, you didn't say Ottercops, did you?"

"Yes, yes," I said, with relief. "Section Officer Ashbee speaking. I wanted to know . . ." There was a pause. "Hullo! Are you there? *Hullo!*"

The voice reappeared, though fainter, and sounding even more puzzled. "Sorry, Ma'am, you mean Ottercops *Moss?*"

"Yes of course, Ottercops Moss. There's only one!" (Thank goodness, I added under my breath.)

"But we thought . . . we thought you were closed!"

"No, *no!*" I almost shouted. "We're still *here!* I wanted to know . . ." then the line went dead.

I rattled and banged the instrument, then groaned. That meant starting all over again. And I hadn't even managed to establish just who it was that I had been talking to, nor how to be sure to get through to them a second time. I made it eventually, unbelievably.

"Hullo. Is that Air Ministry? Ottercops Moss on the line again, Section Officer Ashbee speaking. We got cut off about twenty minutes ago. Can I speak to someone who *knows* about us? Please!"

"Ottercops *Moss* did you say?" It was a different voice.

"Just one moment, Ma'am, I'll see I can find someone."

I clutched my head and pressed the receiver closer to my ear in case I could pick up any muttered asides. Another pause, and yet another voice. "Hullo? Did you say Ottercops Moss? We were under the impression . . ."

"No, *no!*" I interrupted, "We're *not* closed, we're all still sitting here, quite a lot of us. Please, *please* don't forget us. I was ringing because we wanted to know . . ." The line went dead again.

I gave up. But after that I decided to ring at regular intervals, just to make sure that no King's Regulations procedure had been implemented to close the Ottercops Moss file and with it the station itself without our at least knowing.

Meanwhile, the odd visitor to the station did turn up from time to time. A WAAF Code and Cypher Officer came over from our Wing Headquarters, I suppose to check and update that side of things. She and our resident chap, whose senior she must have been in experience if not rank, would then shut themselves up together. Anne was small, rather caustic-tongued, and far more worldly-wise than I was, though we were much the same age. But she had a sense of humour, and once we got together as two girls, we had a few laughs about the awfulness of being shut away, even in so beautiful a corner of the world, with such an impossible selection of the opposite sex. Once we had established a contact, we used to ring each other up every so often to commiserate.

The station was also descended upon by a civilian expert, I think one of those despised "scientific observers," probably for yet another attempt to solve Ottercops's problems with aircraft height identification. He was a much more cultured type than I had had the chance to talk with for ages, and he came with—of all things—an unexpurgated, hard-back edition of *Lady Chatterley's Lover*, goodness knows where or how acquired. It was true contraband in those days.

As luck would have it, he mentioned this when the two of us were alone together and offered to lend it to me first if I'd like to have a look. Of course I said I would! When the others, particularly our obnoxious F/O Engineer, heard that I actually had my hands on it, I was badgered incessantly to hurry up and hand it over. I found myself taking a slightly malicious pleasure in reading it slowly, though I have to admit I couldn't really see what all the fuss was about. After all, the word *fuck*, though never of course seen in print until after the famous *Lady Chatterley* trial, was in constant use by most Other Ranks, and certainly by Airmen.

In the strange atmosphere of suspended animation, punctuated by my anxious phone calls to Air Ministry to remind them we were still there, my mother came up to stay for a few days at the Percy Arms, though how she managed it is, in retrospect, hard to imagine. She came to check up on my state of health because I had collapsed with what they called "a patch on the lung" and had just spent a fortnight in the tiny Sick Quarters on the camp.

It was only afterwards that I realised this must have been a deeply psychological triumph of mind over matter and that "to go sick" was the only way I could escape for a brief respite from my uncongenial companions and situation.

And I was not malingering. I had been really ill, though by the time my mother could arrange to come up, I was pretty well recovered. I would cycle down to Otterburn, and we would chat over a surprisingly "civilized" afternoon tea. I remember the flagged terrace of worn grey stones, and even some spring flowers making a small, brave showing. Wandering by the Otter Burn [river] itself, we caught up with family news.

She herself had been very distressed to learn that my beautiful sister Helen, a violinist, whom I had visited in Chicago three months before the outbreak of war, had left her American husband [Thornton Page], now serving in the US Navy in a submarine. She had taken their little girl [Tanya], with her to New York, where she got herself a menial job in a design studio. Helen was inclined not to write at all unless her life could "be said to be in a respectable state," and the long gaps between her sketchy letters, sometimes due to U-boat activity and not her reluctance to write, gave my mother many sleepless nights.

As regards myself, my mother soon realised how depressed I had been, and still was, at feeling so cut off from "where things were really happening," and she tried to persuade me that I *was* being useful. "They also serve who only stand and wait," as the poet Milton had written, but I didn't really believe her. It was a delightful and unexpected brief interlude though, for we understood each other very well.

She was not long gone from Otterburn before the war began moving towards its final phase, although the first intimation that we had up in Northumberland was an increase in aerial activity. Four and a half years of war had conditioned us to not getting immediate or detailed reports on its course, or of world events. Nor was there any television to show us, even backhandedly, that we were not getting them (such as showing out-of-date stills alongside news readers' faces, a substitute not unknown today).

There was, too, the eternal double dilemma about how not to tell the enemy of the success of their raids while keeping the public informed enough to prevent false reports and rumours from proliferating. In the World War II situation, troops at home or abroad could sometimes be in safer conditions than their loved ones in city centres, so another pitfall for the government purveyors of news was the possibility of "spreading alarm and despondency" by reporting too much.

Though General Eisenhower had announced Italy's unconditional surrender in the September of the year before, 1943, only five days after the first Allied landings in Salerno Bay, the slow struggle to push the

Germans northwards continued, and the Fifth Army did not enter Rome until 4 June 1944.

Two days later I had a free afternoon and decided to cycle down to Otterburn to lie in a little glade I had discovered near the burn itself. As the Scots version of the old ballad said: "The Otterburn's a bonnie burn / 'Tis pleasant there to be." And it was still true, for there is something primevally soothing about the sound of running water. I lay there in the dappled shade, content to open a lazy eye from time to time to glimpse the tufted grasses and small wild flowers, and trying not to think about the waste of it all and, at that moment, this included what I felt to be the waste of my own life.

And then my mind went back again to the battle between the Northumbrian Percy and the Scots Douglas to the moment where the Scots lord knows that he is mortally wounded and says to his page boy:

> "My wound is deep; I fain would sleep!
>   Take thou the vanguard of the three
> And hide me in the bracken bush
>   That grows on yonder lily lea.
> O bury me by the bracken bush,
>   Beneath the blumin' brier
>   Let never living mortal ken
> That a kindly Scot lies there."
>
> He lifted up that noble lord,
>   With the saut tear in his ee;
> And he liid him in the bracken bush,
>   That his merrie men might not see.

Who knew? Perhaps I was lying near the spot where the bracken bush hid the dying Scot from his men so that they should not suffer "alarm and despondency" but would go on fighting?

And then I became aware of another sound, above the faint buzzing of the small forest insects, above the quiet ripple of the brown burn peacefully threading its way through the narrows of pebbles and gravel and around twigs caught up in little foaming bunches. It was the unmistakable drone of bombers, only there had been no air-raid warning. Those were almost things of the past for us now and, anyway, the bombers were flying south. The Second Front must be starting.

I jumped up, hurriedly grabbed my bike, and wheeled it out of the glade and onto the road back up to the camp. I must find out if there was any hard news. Why was I here? Why wasn't I somewhere else where things were happening? I rode, and pushed, and sweated my way back, parked my bike and went quickly into the Officers' Mess. No one there. I hurried round to the Orderly Room.

"Oh, Flight. Seen the CO anywhere?" I asked.

"Not in the Officers' Mess. Ma'am?"

I shook my head. "Not a sign."

"Tried the Sergeants' Mess yet, Ma' am?"

"Okay, okay Flight, I'll do the rounds."

I was just closing the door, when he added: "Oh, by the way Ma'am, Air Ministry was on the line not long ago, wanted a word with you."

"With *me?*"

"Wanted you to ring."

"But I'll never get through now, will I? Something's really happening, isn't it?"

"Looks like it's the balloon going up this time," the Fight said, and a rare smile flickered over his dour features. We both made the thumbs-up sign. It took the usual age to get through; as usual the line went dead several times and I had to start all over again.

At last I seemed to have the right department, but, I thought gloomily, I bet this is where we came in. "Ottercops Moss here," I said, "Section Officer Ashbee speaking. I had a message I was to ring you."

"Did you say Ottercops Moss?" The words came over faintly, but in the all too familiar tone of puzzlement. "But . . ."

Controlling myself so as not to scream I said with an unnatural, icy calm, "That's right. That is precisely what I said . . . one and only Ottercops Moss, I repeat, Moss! The green stuff that grows on stones, or the greyer variety that reindeer eat . . . M-O-S-S, Ottercops! We are not closed!"

There was a pause.

"Just one moment, Ma'am. I'll see if I can find someone."

I held on despairingly, till at last, after a few unnerving clicks, a more authoritative voice said:

"Ashbee? Wing Commander Jones here. Are you there?" "Yessir."

"Now, we know all about you. In fact myself, or someone, will be coming up in a few weeks time to review the whole matter. You'll get a signal. Just carry on as usual. Right?"

"Right, Sir. Thank you, Sir. Oh, and Sir . . ." But the line had gone dead.

———·———

In the middle of that month the first [V-1] flying bombs were dropped on London. They were irreverently called "Doodlebugs" in an instinctive attempt to demystify them, for they were more frightening than the bombing we had got used to. Out of nowhere, there they suddenly were, clattering close and noisily. And the panic element was that you were safe till the noise stopped. When it cut out, the unmanned "thing" could drop anywhere. That was when people started to run. Only they didn't know where to run to. I had a few days leave, and I remember seeing a crowd in London's Oxford Street bumping into each other as the noise stopped and everyone tried to scatter quickly.

In July the attempt to assassinate Hitler failed, the Russians moved westward through eastern Poland, and though I cannot remember in how much detail it was reported, the Warsaw rising began. In the middle of August the British landed on the French Riviera, and suddenly I was back in a magical moment of childhood.

After four years in Jerusalem, my family had been spending the winter months in an unexplored corner of Provence, living more cheaply than would have been possible anywhere else until a future home was found somewhere for the whole family.[1] I was ten, and my sister and I went on an immense expedition with my father to the fortress village of Les Baux.

---

1. See Ashbee's memoir, *Child in Jerusalem* (Syracuse: Syracuse Univ. Press, 2008).

We climbed the cobbled street
Past the *estaminet*,
With lagging dusty feet,
Past marble tables rimmed with gleaming brass,
Safe in dark alcoves from the heavy heat.
(Chicory coffee, black and bitter-sweet,
And thyme-grey honey set in metal pails.)
We reached the castle's crest,
And leaned to rest
On the hot parapet;
And the brown earth lay spread
Hundreds of feet below, the vineyards planned,
The olives planted by some pigmy's hand,
Like silver buttons on the thirsty land.
Now, as the Seventh Army thrusts ahead
Its flying columns sweeping through Provence,
Will Bren-gun carriers shave the hairpin bends
Whipping the dust? Will hob-nailed soldiers tread
The rocky chambers of the inner keep,
And sweating sappers peep
Through loopholes where the feathered arrows sped
At other, long-forgotten, hostile dead?

And before the month was out, Charles de Gaulle entered Paris in the wake of the Allied troops, and Churchill was then rid of his "cross." (He is alleged to have said, "The hardest cross I have to bear is the Cross of Lorraine.")

Meanwhile, the Wingco at Air Ministry was as good as his word. Within a few weeks of our brief phone call, the signal came and some Top Brass duly appeared at Ottercops Moss to start the process of closing the station down. And as a part of that process my posting came through to RAF Stenigot, in Lincolnshire. My love-hate relationship with the fells and the sheep and the Romans was at an end.

9. Southward Ho!

1944–1945

RAF STENIGOT, though another of the first generation of CH Radar Stations, was at least a little nearer civilization, and I felt a lightening of the spirit as the train brought me southwards, finally depositing me in Lincolnshire.[1]

The station had apparently been managing for some time without a WAAF Admin Officer at all; in fact it seemed to have been managing quite adequately. The CO, Flight Lieutenant Brill, was a humorous, go-getting businessman from Leeds who, as a result of a big win on a "halt stake" on the Irish Sweeps before the war, had risen to become the owner of a prestigious and successful gents outfitters. In the absence of a WAAF of officer rank, other than a couple of technical Code and Cypher types, who always tended with a hint of superiority to keep themselves rather apart, he had schooled his various WAAF NCOs into an efficient and friendly team. In fact, the news that a WAAF Admin Officer was going to take over was greeted with something like dismay by the WAAF Admin Corporal Osborne, who had been running things on her own with enjoyment and obvious efficiency.

The CO was fond of the feminine gender, and one of the cosier aspects of this classless and rankless "family" was tea and crumpets together—goodness knows whence acquired—in his office, and quite often. And a

1. In August 1995, during a joint visit by the Society for Lincolnshire History and Archaeology and the Royal Commission on the Historical Monuments of England, Chris Lester photographed the buildings and tower at RAF Stenigot. The ancillary buildings have since been razed, but the surviving transmitter tower, the transmitter building, and the receiver building are Listed for Protection and have not been demolished.

28. Transmitting tower at RAF
Stenigot. Photograph by Chris
Lester, Society for Lincolnshire
History and Archaeology.

rather special "Farewell Crumpet Tea Party" had been arranged to mark
the much lamented ending of this pleasant state of affairs. But the signal
that the Orderly Room had received announcing my arrival had somehow
acquired the wrong date. I turned up the day before I was expected, and
in the surprise of the moment no one could think of any way of preventing
my being ushered straight into the party.

The CO hurriedly took his feet off the desk and stood up, smoothing
his black hair and carefully tailored moustache and emanating the very
best after-shave lotion. He came round the desk and, gold cuff links glint-
ing, extended a well-manicured hand in a disarmingly apologetic greeting. (Jerry Brill was however not one to be at a loss for long.) His WAAF
underlings, quickly gathering their caps and other belongings and the
remains of the crumpet tea, and concealing their resentment as best they
could, made a discreet exit.

I soon found the atmosphere in the Officers Mess marvellously
friendly after Ottercops, and I got quite used to coming in from a Kit

Inspection or a Mess Meeting over which I had to preside to work out the menus for each week, to be offered a drink to the strains of Bach's "Toccata in D" or Sibelius's "Swan of Tuonela," for the CO was a music lover and had brought a lot of his 78s with him.

What he really thought of me, I've no idea (innocent, gullible, but easily manageable, perhaps?), for even after almost five years in the WAAF I was still surprisingly naïve. Some of my colleagues must on occasions have found the "upright" stance I took in the face of irregularities exasperatingly unrealistic. But at least the CO and I could usually laugh together.

Like most of the early radar stations, Stenigot was perched on a hill, the only sizeable one in Lincolnshire. I soon became aware of a different kind of space around me. It was no longer, of course, the Fells, but I had the feeling that there was far more here than there seemed to be in other counties. Standing, looking out from the station, I was aware of the empty hugeness of the sky above me and of the lowness of the distant horizon line.

It was harvest time when I arrived and the fields were golden. The only competition with the bombers going out from nearby RAF Manby was the purr of an occasional distant, tiny scarlet tractor moving backwards and forwards over the landscape, turning the rippling cornfields into fields of stubble, dotted here and there with parcelled stooks.

I quickly established with Corporal Osborne, despite her initial disgust at my arrival, a good and lasting relationship. I learned from her that farmers in this still largely rural area were "doing very nicely thank-you!" She had the most extraordinary tales of prominent locals of the breed inviting a select few WAAF Other Ranks from time to time to lavish (by current wartime standards) *three*-course dinners. These, though decorous enough regarding any actual responses demanded from the WAAF concerned, usually ended with their farmer hosts ritually lighting their cigars with one-pound notes.

This was the stuff of films about the Russian Revolution, calculated to make a pretty startling impact on the minds of some of the WAAF invitees. One-pound notes were still big money at the time. Many of the troops had joined up, voluntarily or by conscription, for the "King's Shilling" which had, granted, by that date risen to *two* shillings a day, fourteen shillings a week. NCOs, of course, got a bit more which they queued up for at the weekly Pay Parade. Pay Parades were done alphabetically and, on all but the tiniest stations, separately for Airmen and WAAF, so while still "in the ranks," I had, as an A, always been lucky and got away with my 14/- quite quickly. Casualties were more frequent amongst the Ws, especially on big stations, and the thuds of fainting WAAF whose names were Watts, White, or Williams were not uncommon occurrences.

PAY NIGHT: (*A query prompted by a certain statue*).

29. Felicity Ashbee. *Pay Night (A query prompted by a certain statue).* "Now ish this an A.T. or a W.A.A.F? Sho difficult to tell without uniformsh." Woodcut. Published in the *WAAF* magazine, February 1940.

Parades of one kind or another were of course an integral part of service life. This was so whether they were Kit Inspections (some very funny things could happen to officially supplied articles of clothing) or inspections of other items of equipment, in the case of the Airmen, of course, weapons. On one occasion the Airmen were summoned for a combined Pay Parade and Small Arms inspection.

The much disliked, miniature Sergeant Dilly lined them up, they cursing under their breaths at not having been given enough time to check that their "small arms" were OK, and swearing that next time they'd stuff him in the nearest water-butt. He then stood them at ease to await the arrival of the officer. It was the rather innocent Technical Officer who was detailed to preside at this particular parade with Corporal Osborne to assist. Though a woman, she was the only available NCO. He entered to Sergeant Dilly's roar of: "Atten-*tion!*" and an intimidating crash of rifle butts and hurriedly laced up boots.

When the officer took his place, he glanced uncertainly at the four-foot-ten-inch Sergeant Dilly on one side of him and the five-foot-ten-inch Corporal Osborne on the other and said mildly, "Now, men, get out your weapons!" It was Corporal Osborne who exploded first. The men quickly followed suit with a roof-raising explosion of laughter.

One of the Airmen had some glandular deficiency which had deprived him of any hair at all. His pink, unlined face was innocent of moustache or even eyebrows, and when bare-headed his scalp had an unbelievable gloss. This he discovered was a Parade-stopping asset. For if he turned his head with a sharp enough jerk when the command was given to, "Eyes . . . *right!*" his forage cap would remain in the front-pointing direction, that is, extending from ear to ear. If the officer or NCO giving the commands was not stage-struck by this phenomenon, the Airman's forage cap would eventually swivel back to its normal position on his smooth head with the command, "Eyes . . . *front!*"

As a station, Stenigot was a fairly small one, which meant that the size of the Parade hall only qualified it for the humblest of ENSA entertainment programmes. ENSA was the only official purveyor of entertainment to camps cut off from access to towns that provided repertory or visiting theatre or concerts, though most camps had at least a hall where Pay Parades were held and visiting films could be shown from time to time.

ENSA entertainments were graded from "A" to "D" or even "E"—"A"s and "B"s being of the kind offered to camps with a large complement of troops of whichever service, and a stage big enough for a sizeable group to perform on. We rated only a "D" or an "E" show, which usually meant a pianist and one instrumentalist or singer. When we were told of a forthcoming ENSA visit, Corporal Osborne was sent round the Nissen huts "beating up" both WAAF and Airmen to make sure there was a reasonable attendance.

"Oh, Corp! Do we have to? What kind of a show is it?"

"Well . . ." Corporal Osborne's loyalties were somewhat divided. "You know, nothing very exciting, a pianist and a soloist I expect, but the new Ma'am will want a good turnout to support them." The Airmen were eventually persuaded by the fact that it wouldn't last too long, and that at least it would be nice and warm.

"Cheaper than an evening at the pub, anyway," Corporal Osborne urged the still reluctant Airmen cheerfully, as she breezed out to the entertainment.

"I bet it'll be one of them goddam awful women yowlin'," one of them muttered. "Long frock an' all too." And he was right.

When the last stragglers had been coaxed into the hall, the performers appeared to some rather muted and desultory clapping. They were a pianist and a lady singer in a long blue frock. The accompanist launched himself manfully into a short introduction and the singer, clasping her hands together, took a step forward. As she opened her mouth to start singing, I became aware of another sound, surely nothing to do with the piano, though its tuning left a good deal to be desired. It sounded more like water, rushing water, quite a lot of water in fact.

> The Princess looked forth from her turreted Tower,
> The horn of the herd-boy rang up from below . . .
> (psh, wsh, wsh, wsh, wsh)
> Oh cease from thy playing and haunt me no more,
> Nor fetter my fancy that freely would soar . . .

(psh, wsh, wsh, wsh, wsh)
When the sun goes down, when the sun goes down . . .
(wsh, wsh, wsh, wsh)

Surely there couldn't be a leak anywhere, could there? There had been no rainstorm. Then to my horror it slowly dawned on me that it must be the automatic flushers on the Airmen's toilets, which no one had thought to switch off. The rushing sound now began to be accompanied by suppressed titters. The words, even without the water accompaniment were to say the least, odd! (What was the audience making of "Nor fetter my fancy that freely would soar?")

I looked wildly round to see if I could catch Corporal Osborne's eye, but I couldn't see her anywhere. It was very difficult for me to leave my prominent position in the front row for my departure might be misconstrued. The singer was launching herself into the second verse, a slightly glazed and rabbitlike look of anxiety spreading over her face. The Princess was still looking out from her Tower, but now:

Mute was the horn that had called from below
Oh why art thou silent, beguile me once more!
(psh, wsh, wsh, wsh, wsh)

If only it *were* silent! There was nothing for it. I must make a dash for the Airmen's toilets and see if anything could be done before the audience's composure was completely disrupted. Stumbling over the front row's feet, I sneaked out to find Corporal Osborne already there, giving moral support to a kneeling Airman who was vainly trying to locate the right valve, or cock, or ball-cock (why *did* plumbing terminology have to be so sexy?) to turn the damn thing off.

"Can't you *do* anything, Smith?" I whispered, crouching down beside him. "There must be *some* way of turning the blasted water off, isn't there?"

"There did oughta be, Ma'am, but I don't seem to find 'er, nowhere's. I dursn't bash 'er too 'ard, Ma'am."

"No, no, quite right, Smith," I interrupted. "We don't want a *real* flood on our hands. We've enough trouble to be getting on with as it is." Meanwhile the Princess went into an anguished third verse.

She wept in the twilight, and bitterly sighed,
(psh, wsh, wsh, wsh, wsh)
What *is* it I long for, what *is* it I long for?
God help me she cried . . .
(psh, wsh, wsh, wsh)

I felt what I needed was help from something a little more immediate and reliable than the Almighty's! Suddenly Corporal Osborne's voice sounded above me, a trifle wobbly with suppressed giggles.

"What's that little tap thing up there?" she asked. She and I both straightened ourselves and peered upwards.

"Could be the cock 'n all?" she suggested.

"Might be worth trying," I said, "if it weren't so high up."

"That's easy, Ma'am. I'll get a chair, Ma'am," Smith said, and he went to locate one in the darkened hall. We heard a crash as he collided with the nearest object. Then he came back clutching an apology for a chair and rubbing his shin. The corporal and I steadied him as he stood up on the less than stable seat. There were a few sweaty grunts, then suddenly, silence.

Into it, from the hall, came a muted cheer, and simultaneously, the song's final line: "And the sun went down . . . the sun went *d-o-w-n*." This was followed by the thunder of Air Force boots and the usual "big hand" for the somewhat surprised soloist. She was probably hardly aware of the extent to which this outburst helped conceal the no longer containable laughter. But having had a bit of fun, the basically friendly audience was quite prepared to be tolerant of the rest of the programme. Who knew? Something else amusing might crop up.

Because of Stenigot's size it was linked with the Bomber Station RAF Manby for certain things, such as doctor and dentist, since we were too small to have resident ones of our own. So when I was smitten with terrible toothache, I was driven over in the small member station van and presented myself and my already swelling face for inspection at the daily dental parade.

"Well, which tooth do you want me to pull out?" the officer asked cheerfully when I had outlined the problem. I pointed dumbly to what I thought to be the offending tooth.

He took another look and shook his head. "Don't think so," he said. "Don't think it's the bottom one. I think it's the one above it. Sometimes the pain is mirrored. Come back again in a couple of days when you're sure. Don't want to pull out two do we?" Brutal, but as it turned out, right.

I endured two more days of increasing agony and finally crept back again to admit that I had been wrong. I then had to explain that local anaesthetics didn't usually take on me, and to ask, would there be any chance of my having gas. The F/O Dental seemed a trifle put out and said he'd have to consult a more senior officer. I stayed sitting in the dental chair, my swollen face propped gingerly in my hand, while he sought higher authority.

Finally he came back with the Wing Commander Dental, a bouncy little chap with a moustache which, though obviously his pride and joy, wasn't quite sure whether it was aping Jimmy Edwards or Salvador Dali.

"Well, Ashbee, you want us to give you gas, do you?"

"If that's all right with you, Sir," I answered. "It's just that, usually, locals don't seem to take on me."

"Depends how they're given," the Wingco replied.

"That's what they all say," I mumbled.

"Well, I daresay we can manage," he said, a little dubiously, after which he and the F/O Dental and the Nursing Sister all got into a huddle together. I waited resignedly, completely unaware that the reason for their hesitation was that the gas equipment was not in very good working order.

"Righty-ho, Ashbee, all set!" the Wingco finally exclaimed, and between them they clapped the apparatus over my nose while offering the usual instructions. I had had gas several times before, and something told me things were not going as they should. I tried to keep my eyes open to show them I was still conscious. Then I heard the alarmingly cheerful remark, "OK. She's off! Carry on!" I felt myself half rise up in the chair as they began the assault on me but then, luckily, I really was "off." The next thing I knew was what seemed to be a flurry of activity around me, including my face being patted and my hands being rubbed and slapped.

"Come along, Ashbee, wake up now!" one of them was repeating somewhat urgently. Then, "Glass of water, quick, nurse," and a muttered curse as the flustered nursing sister dropped it before she could get it back to the Wingco, who presumably intended to throw it over me. I still didn't feel like opening my eyes. What was the hurry about? When I finally did, I thought I caught a distinct sigh of relief.

"I heard you say, 'OK. She's off,' Sir," I said, in what sounded like a rather far away voice. "But I wasn't!"

"But you didn't feel anything?"

"Yes I did, Sir!"

"Well, sorry, too bad." The Wingco responded, slightly huffily. "The gas wasn't functioning. You were having it with God's own air. Quite a feat I can tell you! But you're OK now, what?"

I nodded. "OK, Sir."

"That's a good girl." He patted my shoulder. "And by the way, if any of your lot would like to come over some time, we'll show you around and give you a ride in a Lancaster."[2]

"I'll keep you up to that, Sir!" I said. And I did. We had a very interesting time, too, being shown all the briefing procedures, the maps, and the aerial photographs taken before and after various raids.

"Where was this one then?" I asked, as we bent over the special marked-out plans of some military installation that had been the target for that particular night's attack.

"Königsberg," the young Flight Lieutenant answered. "Long trip that was. This was what we were after." He pointed to a cluster of camouflaged shapes that didn't say much to me.

"And did you knock it out all right?" I asked, almost jokingly, quite unprepared for his reply. "Well, actually . . . no," he said. "We overshot and wiped out quite a bit of residential area by mistake."

I felt my skin prickle. His voice was unemotional, showing neither sadness nor jubilation. They themselves had all come back at least, to go

2. The RAF Lancaster, or "Lanc" or "Lankie," became one of the most famous and successful night bombers of the war. It also excelled in daylight precision bombing and gained worldwide renown as the "Dam Buster" used in the 1943 Operation Chastise raids on Germany's Ruhr Valley dams.

30. The RAF Avro Lancaster B1 bomber.

out and bomb again another night. What had happened was just one of the inevitable consequences of war. You had to put up a guard against feeling these things too much. When we had seen everything they could show us, we went over to the Lancaster standing ready to take us up.

I had no idea that the great towers of Lincoln Cathedral would be so wonderfully near as we rose upwards, nor that the pressure as I stood under the astral dome would force me relentlessly down forwards until I was almost on my knees. A very odd sensation.

"S for Sugar calling! O. K. to scramble?"
"O. K. to scramble!" And we slowly turn
Into the runway, that majestic sweep
Of misty tarmac, straight and dark and firm.

A Titan's roadway, yielding into space
And at the far end, distantly and proud
Lincoln Cathedral rises from the haze;
A burst of music, and a wisp of cloud.

We race the length, we race and lift and soar,
"She's a good kite, she'll show you how to fly!"
And nothing but the curving astral dome
Between me and the sky.

By modern standards the Lancaster was draughty, noisy, and primitive, but at the time it was a trusty stalwart, responsible for innumerable important raids into enemy territory, and these were now increasingly the stuff of the news as the war moved steadily into its later phases.

In September 1944 the Allies captured Antwerp, a slow, muddy, and difficult process; then they liberated Brussels. Though only days after these successes, the first V-2 rocket, alarmingly announced, landed in Britain, and only a week after that came the Arnhem disaster with the heavy casualties which it proved impossible to conceal.[3]

Early in October Churchill spent a week in Moscow and soon after that the Red Army began moving through Romania and on into Yugoslavia, and also in October the Russians and the Yugoslav partisans together entered Belgrade. US troops began landing in the Philippines.

But life for us in our "out-back" went on as before and I had not been long at Stenigot before I found out that Corporal Osborne had started life as a child dancer in pantomime and had gone on to be a qualified instructor in a variety of dance forms, including tap and acrobatic dancing. This was too fortunate a chance not to take advantage of, and the idea was soon born that we put on a show. I called it *Wakey-Wakey*.

Recruits came forward quickly, offering dancing or singing ability or just eagerness to take part, and the lively Corporal Osborne set to mould them into a credible, Folies Bergère–style, high-kicking chorus. This was not an easy task considering the fairly solid shapes that tended to develop from a diet of filling "Woolton" pies, treacle tarts, and suet puddings.

As usual we reused some of my old sketches. And this time I rewrote the "WAAF Officer Selection Board" skit, turning it into its Nazi equivalent which we retitled "Crime Marches On: A Women's Auxiliary Luftwaffe

---

3. This was the British Army's attempt to cross the Rhine, a maneuver intended to last two days that went on for seven before withdrawal became necessary after the forces had suffered many casualties.

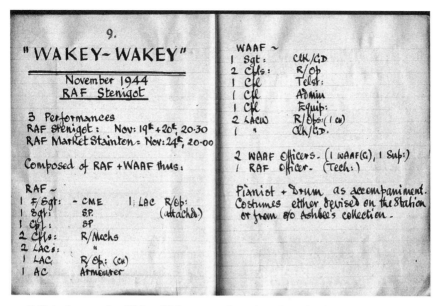

31. Felicity's notes for *Wakey-Wakey*, 1944, from her show log book.

32. Opening chorus for *Wakey-Wakey*, as performed at RAF Stenigot, November 1944.

Board". It had suitably seventeenth-century British Restoration stage names such as Frau Commandant van Blitzen, Frau Boring, and Fraulein Crackling, and an innocent candidate, Corporal Gretchen Ersatz, bossed about by a Sergeant Flannel.

We found some willing musical talent amongst the officers, too, so I dug up a mock opera I had put together for home use before the war. This had a primitive plot of love and jealousy and used most of the really well-known operatic arias. It ended very satisfactorily with a pile of corpses on the stage. Everyone loved it, the more so since the dead were all officers.

As regards solo singers, I found we had a very tolerable baritone in one of our leading Aircraftsmen, and a WAAF Code and Cypher Corporal with a seductively husky alto, just right for a revival of "Corporal Otis Regrets." I also thought she would be well suited to the new skit I'd done on Jimmy McHugh and Harold Adamson's "I Couldn't Sleep a Wink Last Night," from the Frank Sinatra film *Higher and Higher.*

I had no inkling of just *how* "well suited" she would be. For shortly after the show, I was told, to my dismay, that Corporal Freeland was on a charge for being Absent Without Leave, in her case, simply not coming

33. "Crime Marches On: A Women's Auxiliary Luftwaffe Board" from *Wakey-Wakey,* a skit performed at RAF Stenigot, November 1944.

back to camp one night. This was bad enough for a humble Airwoman but much worse when it concerned an NCO and even a couple of stripes were supposed to denote a nodding acceptance of responsibility. The chorus of my parodied version had run:

> The Golden Fleece was warm and light.
> The bar so cosy and bright,
> He said I surely needn't go just yet,
> He said I'd time to finish my last cigarette.
> He told me all about his home,
> And the ice-box that was painted white,
> I still can't understand it happening
> Because I wasn't even faintly tight,
> No, I can't think how I missed the Transport,
> 'Cos I only had a gin last night.

Actually, the second verse was even more apt!

> They've never had me on a Charge.
> I've wriggled out of every plight
> I thought I'd wriggled out of this one too,
> I never thought they'd catch me, but what could I do?
> I said I'd never slipped before.
> I'd always managed quite all right,
> I never thought she'd give me Jankers,
> Because I really wasn't awfully tight,
> Oh, why *did* I miss the ruddy transport,
> When I only had a gin last night!

The trouble was that I was still only a Section Officer, the bottom rank but one in the officer hierarchy, and the punishments that each rank could give were strictly defined. "Jankers" (confinement to barracks) was in many cases all that a junior WAAF Officer could give, and then for not longer than thirty-one days.

It did mean, of course, that the erring WAAF would not be allowed a pass to go away for a precious twenty-four or forty-eight hours during that time, except on extremely compassionate grounds, and that could be a fairly cruel deprivation. The Air Force, and probably also the other services, never came to grips with the problem of punishments for women. There were no women's "glasshouses" (service prisons, as opposed to ordinary civilian ones, in which men in uniform were confined when they really came up against either Air Force or civilian law).

"Jankers" was almost the only thing that a WAAF culprit could be sentenced to. When I realized that I was going to have to take the charge, I felt doubtful that I was senior enough to "make the punishment fit the crime," seeing that it was a Corporal I was going to have to sit in judgment on. If that was what I really felt, then I could do only one thing, remand the charge to a higher ranking officer.

Unfortunately there was no time for me to have a heart-to-heart with Corporal Osborne beforehand, or even get a hint from her—for she was well up in Station gossip—as to the circumstances behind this unfortunate slip on the part of the sultry-voiced ex-member of my cast. And before I had been able to think out any kind of strategy, the disgraced corporal was being marched into my office flanked by two female guards to stand facing me while Corporal Osborne bearing the relevant papers came round to take her place at my elbow.

The accused's hat had already been removed, a time-honoured custom this, to prevent an even worse charge being preferred—insubordination—should he or she be tempted actually to hurl his or her hat at the presiding Officer. What potency as taboo-objects items of headgear always seem to have. Even the unglamorous WAAF peaked cap, or the work-a-day forage cap worn by Airmen, could be transformed into a weapon calculated to start a revolt, or at least bring down the whole edifice of rank.

The charge was read out, then I looked up at Corporal Freeland. An ordinary enough looking girl, straight brown hair with slightly auburn lights, the regulation length neatly rolled so as not to touch the collar. No glamourpuss, though there was a hint of sex appeal to match the sultry voice.

"Have you anything to say, Corporal?" I asked.

"No, Ma'am."

"Can I see her documents, please, Corporal Osborne," I said, barely glancing over my shoulder to where my Admin stood, ramrod straight, holding them. This was the normal procedure for all charges. You heard the charge, listened to the accused's statement, decided on the degree of guilt, and only then looked at the culprit's documents. If there were previous offences, of course, you considered what punishment you would give in the light of these. If judged innocent, the "docs" were not examined at all. If I had looked at Corporal Osborne's face, would I have picked up the message she afterwards claimed she was urgently trying to convey to me? I doubt it. It would have been a far too complicated one to get across on glances alone. Station gossip tended to be rather involved.

As it happened, Corporal Freeland's docs were unblemished. But nonetheless I felt that as a corporal, she oughtn't to get off with the light sentence which was all that I could mete out to her. She was supposed to "set an example," wasn't she? The parodied words of the song she had brought the house down with, came back to me:

> They've never had me on a charge,
> I've wriggled out of every plight,
> I thought I'd wriggle out of this one too,
> I never thought they'd catch me, but what could I do?

I looked up at her. Was the silence a little unnatural. "Well, if there are no extenuating circumstances, and you have nothing to add, Corporal," I said, pausing (for a confession?), "I'm afraid I shall have to remand you to the Station Commander."

Normally, when I remanded charges to the CO it was I who had to stand at his side, holding the docs in readiness, as Corporal Osborne had stood at mine. But by some convenient technicality, and without my knowledge, it was somehow arranged that I should not have to be present. I did not manage to see the accused on her own either, so it was a complete shock to me when I learned that the CO had dismissed the charge.

I nearly exploded.

"But Ma'am," Corporal Osborne bleated, struggling to retain a vestige of appropriate composure. "I was trying hard to stop you!"

"What do you mean, to stop me? You didn't say a thing!"

"I was willing you not to remand it to the CO. You must have felt it. That first one, the blonde you remanded just after you'd arrived, I put that down to your not knowing the ropes or the CO. But now, didn't you know? Everyone knows!"

"Knows *what?*"

"That that the CO and Corporal Freeland were . . . are . . . having an affair! He's been through several others already, this is just the first brunette."

"Corporal Osborne," I almost shouted.

"But, Ma'am!"

By this time any question of "proper respect for rank" had vanished, and Corporal Osborne was dissolving in a nearly hysterical mix of tears and laughter. But I was still too angry to see the funny side of it.

"Everyone knows!" Corporal Osborne repeated. "It's just that they've . . . that he's . . . usually managed to get away with it before. I don't know who spilt on him this time. Bit of the green-eyed, I expect."

"I can't believe it." I said. "It was only two days ago, he was assuring me he'd never been unfaithful to his wife," though I suddenly remembered the slightly soppy look on his face as he told me.

Corporal Osborne exploded again into her now very sodden handkerchief. "And you, you believed him? Oh Ma'am, Ma'am!" The laughter she was no longer able to control was not against me, not derisive. We laughed a lot together, for we seemed to find so many things that happened so extremely funny. It was just that it was difficult for her to believe that someone several years older than herself, with other kinds of "life experience," could be so incredibly naïve when it came to human fallibility. I found myself starting to join in her laughter.

"Well, there's nothing to be done about it now, anyway," I said. "Perhaps the CO will restrain himself a bit more in future."

"Some hope." The words were half smothered in wet handkerchief. "Oh, by the way, Ma'am, there's another charge coming up. It's going straight to the CO. This time you'll have to be there."

"What's this one for?"

"Insubordination."

"Oh, dear! Who on earth is it?"

"LACW [Leading Air Craft Woman] Watkins, Ma'am."

"Watkins! Good God! But has she enough wits to be insubordinate? There aren't that many wits there, are there? No offence meant, of course, poor old Watkins!"

"I think Sergeant Dilly accused her of not scrubbing the cookhouse floor properly, and she cut up rough."

The CO was conveniently not in the Mess that evening, or we might have had some rather sticky moments. By the time we met to sit in judgment on Watkins, I had sorted out my reactions and greeted him with what I hoped was a suitably mature, even cynical expression.

"Hullo Ash," he said brightly. "Now, what's all this about?"

"Out of my hands, Sir. Insubordination. She's all yours."

"Oh Lord," he groaned, as I took up my position, standing at his elbow. There was a sound as of a scuffle outside, and the door opened. Corporal Osborne, obviously only barely in control, but with the help of two suitably stalwart WAAF guards, propelled the insubordinate form of the cookhouse miscreant into the room.

Finally, the hatless though turbaned Watkins (had she been wearing the curlers and turban under the hat before it was forcibly removed?) stood glowering in front of the CO at his seat of judgment, and the charge was read out. There was quite a lot of it. "Now Watkins," said the CO, looking up from the charge sheet. "Have you anything to say?"

"Yessir, I 'ave, Sir!"

"Well, what is it, Watkins?"

"It's me veins, Sir!"

"Your *what?*" said the CO, genuinely startled.

"Veins, Sir, me *veins!*"

And with an unexpectedly acrobatic movement, the solid Watkins heaved one leg up onto the CO's desk with a crash. The crash was the greater because cookhouse personnel still wore old-fashioned, wooden-soled clogs to preserve their feet from floors chronically sodden with water or grease.

It was true. The leg in question was a fine specimen of knotted varicose veins, displayed by an equally dexterous tug to the lisle stocking and the clog which, had the idea occurred to Watkins, was a weapon capable of doing quite a bit of damage. But discretion being the better part of valour when the charge was insubordination, the CO merely drew back an inch or two from the proffered evidence and allowed the culprit to tell her tale in full.

"I've always done me work proper, Sir, and them what says I 'aven't's lyin' in their teeth, Sir, if they got any. It's just them dratted veins, Sir. They don't 'arf draw. Me other leg's just as bad. I can show you."

"All right, Watkins, I'll take your word for it," the CO said hurriedly.

I was careful not to catch Corporal Osborne's eye but stood waiting, holding the "docs" in readiness.

"Is that all, Watkins?"

"Yessir."

"Right. You may remove the evidence."

"Sir?"

"Put your leg down, Watkins."

"Yessir!"

Leg and clog were withdrawn from the table, nearly sweeping the COs wire in-tray off at the same time. I caught it with one hand and with the other proffered him Watkins's docs. He glanced at them, then looked again at the bulging lumpish form which no amount of kitchen soap could ever rid of the faint smell of frying animal fat.

"Watkins," he said.

"Sir?"

"I'm going to dismiss this charge, but, now listen carefully. That cook-house floor has got to be spotless . . . and that means *whenever* I think to come in and take a look at it. Understood?"

The unbeautiful, middle-aged face relaxed with a disbelieving smile. "You bet, Sir! Bless you, Sir!"

"Right. Corporal Osborne. Charge dismissed."

Did I catch a glint of amusement in the corporal's eye as she wheeled the party out and we heard them clump off back to the Orderly Room? Perhaps dismissing charges was becoming a habit?

———•———

Small stations have their compensations to make up for the snags of iso-lation and lack of facilities. Christmas 1944 was quite a cheerful feast at

Stenigot. Crossing the rough little spinney between the Huts and the Mess in the Christmas Eve dusk, I met Corporal Osborne, who gave me such a smashing Parade Ground salute that she tripped over a root and fell flat on her face, thus missing my equally stylish response. Helping her up, and contributing a handkerchief to the cleaning up process, gave us both time to get over our helpless laughter.

There was a chance for a little simple fun, too, in spite of the news our crackling wireless sets gave us of the "Battle of the Bulge," which had begun in the Ardennes the week before, and of the Russians, whose relentless sweep westwards brought them to the outskirts of Budapest by 27 December. By the middle of January 1945, they had reached Warsaw and Cracow, though U-boats, now using homing torpedoes, were taking a fresh toll of British shipping in the Atlantic.

The memory of Stenigot's last winter lingered on. It had been shockingly cold, and the camp had been more or less snowed up for weeks. There had even been an occasion when a double-decker bus had been stuck in a snowdrift and all the passengers had had to be accommodated on the station for the night.

The water supply to most of the WAAF and Airmen's huts froze up, and much time had to be spent melting down chunks hacked from the surrounding snowdrifts to get enough water for even perfunctory washing let alone the filling of the hot-water bottles of those lucky enough to have such sissy luxuries. An hour and a half's refilling of saucepans with snowballs barely filled one hot-water bottle, assuming of course you had been able to keep the hut stove going with the coal conveniently coaxed through the netting round one of the camp's coal stores. (Nuffield STs smeared with Ronuk floor polish were wonderful starters to recalcitrant Nissen hut stoves.)

Added to which there had been what amounted to a veritable plague of rats. When the WAAF went on duty, particularly at night, posses of Airmen with cudgels had had to be mustered to escort them and protect their legs from attack. The rats were only finally got rid of by having all the huts fumigated with some pretty potent kind of gas. Unfortunately one of the WAAF, on returning from leave, missed out on the information and went straight to her hut. Of course, she quickly succumbed and was rescued only just in time.

Meanwhile, as far as I personally was concerned, the wheels of promotion, though grinding exceeding slow, had reached me, and a signal came through that I was now a Flight Officer. This automatically meant a posting, and towards the end of January I found myself sewing an extra stripe onto the cuffs of my uniform jacket and onto the epaulettes of my greatcoat. The next thing I knew I was on my way to what was to be my last posting, the Cradle of the Air Force: RAF Cranwell.

10. Winding Down

1945

IT WAS IN FEBRUARY 1945 that I arrived at RAF Cranwell.[1] At about the same time, Roosevelt and Stalin sat down together at the Yalta Conference to plan Nazi Germany's unconditional surrender. British troops were reaching the Rhine on a ten-mile front, General Douglas MacArthur was entering Manila in the Philippines, and massive air raids on Tokyo were just beginning.

Cranwell was a very different kettle of fish from the last three stations I had been on, all of which had been small. Here I was one of forty-five WAAF officers of all various trades and professions. We were in a couple of the larger peacetime brick houses, which by their sizes must have been for the most senior officers and their families.

We had a dozen or so Code and Cyphers, Medical Officers, Accountants, Equipment and Catering Officers as well as us, the Admin types. There were some half dozen or so of us and we were already beginning to get memos from on high about the first steps in the incredibly complicated business of the return to civilian life. Just how the gradual winding down process was to be initiated and organised, and what our role in it as Admins was to be, began only to emerge as the days and weeks passed.

I set to work acclimatising myself to being one of a team again, which I had not been since Middle Wallop after my initial transfer from Intelligence to Administration, and it took a bit of getting used to after the

---

1. RAF Cranwell still operates as a training base. It hosts the RAF College, the Directorate of Recruiting, and the No. 3 Flying Training School. Other units provide training functions for the Air Cadets, non-RAF Armed Forces personnel, and military personnel from abroad.

34. College Hall, RAF Cranwell, 2010. Photograph by Chris Lester, Society for Lincolnshire History and Archaeology.

chummy, almost family atmosphere of Stenigot. But I was very busy from the word go because the Squadron Officer Admin, known to all as "Squoff" Owen, who seemed to me to be quite an old woman, was soon to be discharged herself and was obviously not interested in detail. Actually she was an unusual and courageous woman who had lived in Spain through much of the Spanish Civil War (between 1936 and 1938). In spite of marital difficulties she had borne and reared five children, the eldest of whom was a much-decorated Pathfinder Squadron Leader.

She was only too glad to let me get on with things and handle the problem cases that came up without constant reference to her. These were usually to do with pregnant WAAF whose condition was often only discovered in the sixth or seventh month of their pregnancy. It was a continual surprise what a WAAF uniform, even battle dress and trousers, could conceal. By then there was precious little time left to get the unmarried mother-to-be fixed up somewhere to have her baby. Usually it had to be one of the voluntary societies, most of them religious, who retained a Victorian censorious moral attitude as often as not, totally insensitive to the circumstances in which the girls had "got themselves into trouble."

I remember one girl, a lively, north-country, Gracie Fields type, a Telephonist in her late twenties who confessed to her pregnancy only at nearly six months, and then very reluctantly. Having found out that she was not a Catholic, I was about to word the letter to the Church of England Society asking for their help when it transpired that it was not her first slip. The details I had to give made this difficult to conceal, but when the reply came from the Society that as it was the girl's second "fall" they would not consider taking her into any of their Homes for Unmarried Mothers, I was enraged. Where was she to go to have her baby? I was faced with a huge problem of finding any harbourage for her at that late stage.

And there was the sad case of Groves, one of the many humble ACWs from the cookhouse, whose overweight, lumbering form concealed her condition almost until the last moment. When she was finally forced into admitting that she was probably eight months pregnant, I blenched slightly and said, "Now Groves, tell me what you can. There isn't much time, you know. And we have the baby to think of, don't we."

Silence.

"What about the father? Are you in touch with him?"

Still silence.

"Is he on this station?"

A slow, almost imperceptible shake of the head.

"But you do know who it was?"

Silence.

"If you would tell me just a little bit about him we could try and get in touch with him for you."

"'Sno good, Ma'am. You wouldn't find 'im, and 'ee wouldn't do nothin', neither."

"What about your own family? Do they know?"

Another shake of the head. "Me Mam's dead."

"I'm sorry. And your father? What about him?"

"'E'd murder me. Bringin' shame on 'im, like . . . you see Ma'am, *him*, me man . . ." (there was almost a wistful lingering on the word), "'e were black."

But once the words had been said, we got on a little faster. I even managed to raise a flicker of a smile on her poor, cowed features. And at least there were no overtly racist questions to be answered on the forms for the Voluntary Societies. We were only at the start of the mixed-race baby boom then. But that didn't mean I would actually find somewhere that would take Groves in on time. I wrote off to a couple of the Societies, and an urgent letter to the Air Ministry as well. When I had a lukewarm, almost casual response from the latter, I decided I couldn't risk waiting, and Squoff Owen not being around, probably on leave, I went in to beard the RAF Admin Wingco Cormandy.

"Well, Ash, what's the trouble?" he asked, as I came in, clutching the offending Air Ministry letter, and saluted.

"I need your help, Sir," I said. "It's about a *very* pregnant WAAF, and Air Ministry's being impossibly complacent."

"In what way, Ash?"

"Well, just take a look at these letters, Sir."

I spread them out in front of him on the desk and waited while he read them. He was a small, rather humourless, slightly conventional man, with greying hair and a neatly groomed moustache.

"Well, Ash, I'm not quite clear what you want *me* to do about it? A little off my beat, don't you think? What?"

"But Sir, I . . . we . . . *you* can't just leave it at that, Sir! Look at the date on their letter! She's over eight and a half months! I need back-up from you, an urgent phone call at least."

"I don't quite see how I can be of any use to you, Ash," he said, fingering his tie in some embarrassment, as he held out the letters to me.

"OK, Sir, if that's your last word? But don't say I didn't warn you!"

I picked up the letters, saluted smartly and turned towards the door. As I opened it I added, "If the baby's laid in your 'in' tray, Sir, think of the headlines! BLACK BABY FOUND IN WING COMMANDER'S . . ."

"What?" shouted the Wingco. "Come back, Ash! Shut the door! Did you say . . . black?"

"Yes, sir! I thought I'd mentioned it . . . black."

It was a bit unfair! But I felt that only shock tactics would help at this eleventh hour. And of course they did.

Another case that I had a lot of difficulty with—though this was not until later in the year—was a girl from Huddersfield who through a bit of Orderly Room inefficiency was suddenly found to have been Absent Without Leave for three months. When the mistake was finally discovered, the

RAF Special Police were sent to her home to arrest her and bring her back to camp.

She stood before me, hatless, grubby, pitiful. When the charge had been heard and I had given her the maximum punishment, seeing that, though only partially her fault, a three-months absence almost amounted to desertion, I had her back in to find out what on earth had really been going on.

"Sit down, Williams. Take off your hat. That's better. Cigarette?"

"Oh, thank you, Ma'am."

"Now let's hear the whole story."

It turned out that she had gone home on her normal leave to find the family in disarray. Her mother had left home, the father was working long factory hours on war work of some kind, and there was no one to look after a young teenage sister and a little brother. When Williams's leave had come to an end, she had asked for an extension on compassionate grounds. She was given another fortnight but had not known how to handle things when, on asking for a second extension, it was refused. It was then that the Orderly Room had slipped up, and when she heard no more, she simply stayed home looking after the family, vaguely hoping for the best.

She had been a cotton spinner before call-up, and now that the war was nearing an end, many skilled workers were being invited to go back into their previous jobs. Williams was obviously of far greater use at home, keeping her young siblings off the streets and working in a textile mill at a job she was skilled at, than scrubbing floors as an ACW/GD [Air Craft Woman/General Duties] at Cranwell.

"Now Williams, listen," I said. "I will write straight to Air Ministry to state the case for your Compassionate Release. Does the firm you used to work for want you back, do you know? Can you give me all the details?"

"Oh yes, Ma'am. I went to see the boss when I was at 'ome. 'E'd be glad to 'ave me back."

"Good. But you'll have to be patient. It'll take a bit of time, and meanwhile you'll have to stay here. Have you anyone in Huddersfield who can help with your sister and little brother?" She thought she might be able to call on a neighbour or two if they knew it wasn't for long.

"I have to trust you absolutely, Williams," I added.

"Oh, Ma'am, you can, truly."

The letter with her case described in detail went off the next day, and within a fortnight the answer came: "Insufficient grounds for a Compassionate Release." I was furious! What insensitive idiot in an office far from the scene of action had not bothered to read my arguments properly?

I tried a second time, with the same result. What could I do now? By this time Williams's plight had become for me a matter of principle. The only thing I could think of was to get a question asked in the House. I had heard, in theory, of such a measure being very effective, but how on earth did one achieve it in practice? Obviously I would have to start by finding out who the MP for Williams's part of Huddersfield was. Fortunately, and not surprisingly, seeing that the Labour government had just got in with its huge majority, Huddersfield was represented by Labour in the person of Joseph P. W. Mallalieu (1908–1980).[2] I collected handfuls of half crowns, florins, shillings, and sixpences and crept out of camp to find a call box at what I hoped would be a time when I might catch an MP in the House. Presumably I would have to make it a personal call.

Of course it took ages, but eventually I got as far as Westminster, and then there was a snag. The MP for Huddersfield East was apparently not available.

"Oh, please," I said urgently to the operator, "could you ask just where he is at the moment. It's very important." And then by one of those lucky breaks I heard the whole conversation between the operator and the MP's secretary, including the number where he could be reached.

I went back in to camp to get some more change, then out to the call box to start all over again. And I got him. And he was terribly nice.

I explained that I was in a call box outside the confines of RAF Cranwell and was doing something that might get me court-marshalled if it came out, though I'd give him my name if he wanted it. Also that I might run out of small change.

---

2. Long a prominent member of the Labour Party, Mallalieu served in several governments and was knighted.

"Give me your number there, and if we're cut off I'll call you back," he said. When I'd got to the end of the Williams story, I said, "So I thought . . . couldn't you ask a question in the House?"

"It's a possibility," he said with what sounded over a rather crackling wire like a hint of amusement. "But I think I'll have to see the girl personally, first. Can you get her down to me?"

"Of course. Easily. Just say when, and I'll give her a forty-eight-hour pass and full instructions! There's only one thing. Can you see she's all right? I mean, she's never been to London before."

"Not to worry." he said. So we fixed the date and the time and the place, and next day I called Williams in, swore her to secrecy, and gave her the plan of campaign with enough money for her return fare and some extra for possible emergencies. People were used to sitting up all night in mainline railway stations in those days, and Williams was not daunted at the thought that that was what she might have to do. I told her though that her MP might offer help of some kind, and that I was sure she could trust him.

Actually, he never did ask that "Question in the House." Apparently, taking it up with Air Ministry, and the mere suggestion that an "ill question" might result if no action were taken, was enough to make them reexamine my two turned-down applications. Williams's compassionate discharge came through in a couple of weeks. We had an almost tearful farewell. I've often wondered what happened to her. After the war was over, I wrote to Mallalieu and thanked him properly, and I had a very nice tea with him at the House.

But before all that, even before the excitement of the General Election, I had of course got bitten with the idea of putting on another show. We did three separate performances, two at Cranwell and one at nearby RAF Swinderby. And on the first Cranwell night we had the services of the RAF College orchestra, conducted by none other than the RAF College's Director of Music, Flight Lieutenant George Sims himself. A well-built, cheerful, and friendly little man, he later rose to the rank of Wing Commander in charge of all the RAF bands.

The sketches included some of the hardy perennials, updated to fit the current mood, and a couple of new ones. One of these, drawing on my Stenigot experiences of the WAAF Corporal who was the CO's "popsey," was Americanized with film-star allusions and what we had picked up of Yankee slang. The entire cast chewed gum all the time. We called it *Lease-Lend*.

And as usual, there were the latest "popular numbers" to make parodies of. The last item was again my mock Victorian melodrama, "The Fall of the House of Shudderbottom," which never failed to hit the bulls-eye.

———•———

But events in the great world outside the camp were beginning to move with extraordinary speed. On 12 April 1945, in the middle of our last rehearsals, Franklin Roosevelt died, and the American presidency passed to Harry Truman. Exactly a fortnight later came the historic meeting of the Russian and the American forces at Torgau.

Then on 28 April, two days after our third performance, Mussolini was killed by the Italian partisans, and on 30 April came the unbelievable news of Hitler's death in the bunker. It seemed almost inconceivable. We had lived with the threat and the evil of his presence for so long, for so many years. Could it really be true? Had he really, at last, been obliterated from the world stage? We had no television, and practically no personal wireless sets, so everyone was glued to the one in the Mess.

Only two days later the city of Berlin surrendered to the Russians, and the next day, 3 May, the Allies entered Hamburg, and on the other side of the world, on the day after that, Rangoon. On 7 May, General Jodl made the final capitulation of Germany to General Eisenhower near Rheims. And on 8 May, von Keitel finally surrendered to Zhukov near Berlin, and "VE" day was proclaimed.

The atmosphere of expectation had been so great that, according to the *Times* of 8 May, crowds had begun assembling early during the day before, just standing around in the streets, particularly in London, waiting for official news. Already that evening tens of thousands were singing and dancing outside Buckingham Palace, shouting at intervals for the King. In the outlying districts some of the time must have been spent in collecting wood for the countless bonfires that ringed London, bursting into flame as soon as the actual announcement came. Also, in fixing up the floodlighting of buildings, the "girls" of the ATS were responsible for St. Paul's itself. That sudden switching on of the lights was symbolic.

Churchill broadcast at 3 p.m. on Tuesday 8 May 1945 announcing that hostilities would "end officially" at one minute after midnight. King George VI spoke at 9 p.m., after which the Royal Family appeared several times on the balcony of the palace, and just before midnight, the two princesses were allowed to go down with their escorts and mingle with the crowd. It was thought that in Trafalgar Square the numbers rose from 60,000 to 100,000 before anyone even contemplated going home.

There must have been some dreadfully compelling reasons of duty—though I can't remember what they were—that prevented my getting down to London for the great celebrations, though a partial deterrent might have been that I no longer had any friends or relatives there with whom I could have stayed for what was left of the night, once the revelry was over.

My Accountant Officer friend Irene [Swift, later, Murphy] (she had been a stalwart in several of the sketches in the show), was visiting another station, RAF Silverstone, and was there on the Sunday when the piecemeal capitulation began to be reported. Tuesday would be a day of national celebration. A party sprang up spontaneously—as must have happened on stations all over the country—with wild tangos being performed. Irene danced with a flower between her teeth.

From that day on, of course, it became harder and harder to keep up any feelings of patriotic fervour or urgency. Fortunately though, the sense of almost total anticlimax was mitigated by the run up to the General Election which started less than three weeks after VE day.

The "gutter press," though I don't think we called it that then, went to town on the Conservative side with the accusation that if Labour won they were going to bring in a Gestapo state in Britain. This in turn was countered by the then-famous phrase "Whose finger on the trigger?" which didn't do Churchill's image as a suitable premier for peacetime much good.

I had never voted before, though I was eligible just in time for the last election before the outbreak of war. But in my home area there were only the dark blue rosettes of the Tories or the pale blue ones of the Liberals to choose between, and I didn't want either! So as yet I had never exercised my democratic right.

Now, it was all enormously exciting, though I have to confess I can't remember just how we in the Services at home put the fateful crosses on our voting papers that July 5th. I think all Service personnel had postal votes because so many of them were still thousands of miles from any electoral roll on which they might originally have been registered, let alone all the six–years' worth of new citizens of voting age, as yet unregistered.

We WAAF officers, all forty-five of us, were still living together in the same houses to which I had clocked in on arrival six months earlier. As the results began to come in, more and more of those favouring the Tories gathered in gloomy disbelieving groups, or sank dejectedly into the floral linen upholstery of the sagging sofas and heavy armchairs of the sitting room. Clutching whiskies or gin-and-tonics, they looked despairingly at each new member of the Mess as she came in with yet another lost seat to report, repeating in a sort of Greek chorus: "But it's not possible!"

"It *can't* be! Not Billericay?" (or Bromley, or Norwich, or Winchester, or whatever Conservative stronghold had fallen.)

I always reckoned it was a very real example of democracy. "The People" went out in their hundreds of thousands, all over the country, to cheer Churchill for having "led the Nation to Victory," for having "beaten 'old 'Itler'" and then, having said their heartfelt "thank-yous," in many cases with real affection, they went quietly home and voted for Attlee. The Conservatives completely misunderstood this. Many of them took it to be a betrayal of the great man, a kick in the teeth for the Saviour of the Nation. Almost all my WAAF officer colleagues misinterpreted what was happening in just that way. But it was nothing of the sort. The British people were merely much more politically mature than they were given credit for. It seems they felt they knew that the kind of leader you want to win a war for you is not necessarily the same as the one you want at the helm for the peace that is to follow. Finally Irene and I could stand the atmosphere no longer. We were apparently the only two WAAF Officers to have voted Labour. We glanced at each other, then sidled as inconspicuously as possible towards the door. Once outside we breathed a sigh of relief, then burst out laughing before hurrying away to some more cheerful place to listen to the rest of the results as they came in.

It took three weeks for the full vote count to be completed, and only on 26 July was Labour's landslide victory official.

Eleven days later, on 6 August, the first atom bomb was dropped on Hiroshima, and on 9 August, the second one on Nagasaki. Eight days after that Japan finally surrendered, which event was in its turn celebrated by "VJ" day.

Irene had gone to bed very early that night and was woken by someone banging on her door shouting "VJ! VJ!" She got up and dressed hurriedly and ran to the big Mess where a party was already in progress with the Cranwell band playing. Nurses from the local hospital had come and joined us, and as the evening progressed everyone moved outside and started to process round the camp, the band leading. By this time Irene had managed to persuade the drummer to let her have a go on the big drum.

This repeat celebration, though nationwide, was rather more muted than "VE" had been. Nevertheless, there are quite a few people born in the mid 1940s called Victor or Victoria, who were conceived during those two joyful May and August nights of celebration.

But war-ending or not, there we all still were, going on with our Clothing Parades, our Church Parades, our Kit Inspections, and our Orderly Room procedures with their Standing Orders, for there were still between six and seven hundred WAAF, not to mention Airmen, on the station strength, however restive they might have been getting.

It must have been around then, if not a little earlier, that the rules about WAAF applying for discharge were altered again. At the peak of manpower (and womanpower) shortage, girls could only apply for discharge if they were pregnant. Now the rules were changed back again to what they had been earlier in the war, and they had only to show proof of marriage.

I discovered that no one had kept any easily accessible visual records of which WAAF were single and which married, so I proceeded to find out, and to all the little cards, in their groups of trades and sections, slotted into a huge wallboard behind my desk, I added a small, neat red square to the name of each married WAAF. I also started a new and much more detailed card index, not only of new arrivals to the station, but of WAAF already with us. This had space for new information about what they had done before joining up (if they were old enough to have done anything) and what ideas—if any—they had about a return to "civvy-street."

The Wingco Admin breezed into my office soon after these colourful additions had been made to my records. "Hullo, Ash," he said.

"Hullo, Sir, anything I can do for you, Sir?"

"Just lookin' in to see how you were doin', Ash. Colourful display you've got there. What's it in aid of?"

"Well, Sir, I thought it would be useful to know how many of the WAAF were married."

"Married? Why do we need to know that, Ash?"

"Well, Sir, all they need to show when they apply for discharge now, Sir, is marriage lines."

"Good God! That so? I thought they had to be, er, had to get, er . . ."

"Sorry, Sir, I'm afraid you're out of date. All the bumpf's through from Air Ministry."

"Good God! You mean to say all those names with little red squares on 'em are married women?"

"I'm afraid so, Sir. If they want to get out now, it's easier to get spliced, and unspliced again afterwards, than to get pregnant and then not be able to get rid of the baby."

"Oh come, Ash!" the Wingco twiddled his moustache in remembered embarrassment, "Mustn't say things like that. Not really as bad as that, is it?"

"I just thought it would be a good idea if we knew, Sir. That was all."

Not long afterwards the Flight Lieutenant Signals paid me a call. "Hullo, Ash," he said, "I hear you're keeping some colourful records these days."

I was on the phone and waved a hand towards my red-spotted board, with a special tap on the section concerning signals clerks and telephonists.

"And what do the little red squares mean, did you say?"

"They mean they're married and can apply for discharge." "Good Lord! But, that's . . . that's . . ." he made a quick calculation, "that's two-thirds of my section's strength," he said, unbelievingly.

"That's right. Marry today, apply for discharge tomorrow," I said airily.

"But, I thought . . . I thought they had to be . . . er . . ."

"That's what the Wingco thought too. But I'm afraid you're both of you out of date. Not been reading your Air Ministry Orders carefully enough. Proof of splicing is all you need now."

"Good Lord!" he repeated in a slightly dazed way.

After that there were quite a few taps on my door by people coming in to check up on my famous board as to the likely future of their sections.

11. And OUT!
1945–1946

MEANWHILE THE MEMBERS OF MY OWN FAMILY were scattered over various parts of the country, not to mention sister Helen still in America. Godden Green, the big family home in Kent, which had been commandeered by the Army on my father's death in 1942, had not yet been derequisitioned.

My mother had at first been staying nearby, and then living with my elder sister, Mary, in Marlborough to help when her second child [Francis] was born. They had at once been asked to "find other accommodation," for many people forced to let their spare rooms drew the line at children. Mary's third child [Richard] was due in January 1945, and warning noises were already being made by their current landlady about not being able to keep the family after the event, which as it happened was pretty traumatic.

It was a bitter January in many parts of the country, and Marlborough was under deep snow. The hospital was some distance from where they were living, and there was no available ambulance service. When Mary's time came, her husband, Ted, who had arrived on compassionate leave from Yatesbury, went next door to phone for the member of the Women's Volunteer Service who was supposed to be ferrying them to the hospital, only to find that the system had broken down and no one was available. In the end, the two of them had to walk in the dark in deep snow to the hospital in Savernake Forest, Mary already in labour. They came to no harm, however, and both mother and baby Richard were soon reported to be "doing well." To start with, at least. But nobody realised that the four-year-old Olivia had contracted measles at her play group, and before it was diagnosed she and the one-year-old Francis were brought to visit the new baby brother in hospital and the whole family came down with the

158

disease as soon as mother and child came home. This was the signal for the landlady to give them notice to quit.

The Charity Commission, for which Ted worked before he was called up, had been evacuated to Morecambe in 1939. It had stayed there throughout the war, and there was a distinct possibility that, come the peace, it might remain there. Mary was still in touch with the wives of some of Ted's colleagues, and they wrote that houses up there were going cheap. So a decision was taken, and before things became impossible in Marlborough my mother found and bought a small house in Hest Bank, midway between Morecambe and Lancaster. She, Mary, and the three children moved there in the spring of 1945, and Ted got a commission as a Met Officer around that time. He was soon posted to one of the East Anglian airfields and was able to snatch the odd forty-eight hours to visit his family.

Horst, with his Pioneer Corps detachment, had been moved from the Forest of Dean and, in spite of their status as noncombatants, which precluded their being used in any proximity to military action, had been sent to France in the wake of the Second Front. Their duties were connected with the War Graves Commission,[1] and they were supposedly unarmed, though they were issued rifles, and if by bad luck they had come into direct contact with the German army they wouldn't have stood much of a chance. Indeed on one occasion Horst almost came to grief. He had been doing some sketching of the Normandy scenery, his rifle propped beside him, and had not noticed that he had been left behind by his platoon, when suddenly he found himself caught up in the platoon's action. He made an undignified bolt for it, his precious water-colour paint box in one hand, his nearly forgotten and incriminating .303 in the other.

Meanwhile, my sister Prue and five-year-old Conrad moved back to London, where Prue found them a room. Unfortunately Prue and Horst's enforced separation led, the following year, to the breakdown of their marriage. This happened in many unions where one or other of the partners simply could not withstand the double pressure of coping alone while

---

1. A private commission that registered the names of those lost and buried in France.

trying to handle new friendships in disrupted and difficult living conditions with rationing and other wartime shortages.

The marriage of my sister Helen and her American husband, who by this time was serving with the US Navy working on sonar detection systems in submarines, had suffered a similar fate, and Helen was already living in New York with five-year-old Tanya and a new companion.

My mother, who had steered her own by no means always easy partnership with my father through some very rough patches, at first found these breakdowns in the marriages of two of her children hard to accept. The more so as she had taken these two different sons-in-law very much to her heart, particularly the German one, whose refugee status she and my father had guaranteed from 1937 and whose future, including his ultimate nationality, was still by no means clear.

After VJ day, the number of WAAF Officers on the strength at Cranwell began to diminish noticeably, and there was no longer any need for a separate WAAF Officers' Mess, so we were all moved into the main RAF Mess building. This meant that the dining room, sitting (or "ante") rooms, and bar were turned over to mixed sex use, a much more satisfactory situation for all. The fact that gossip (even scandal) about who was getting off with whom could be discreetly discussed while propping up the communal bar merely added spice to the situation.

"Don't look now, but did you see who's just come in with old so and so?"

"Good Lord! So it is. Well, well. But did you notice who was sitting at breakfast this morning with that little blonde Code and Cypher bit?"

"You *can't* mean old . . . ?"

"I can, you know."

"Well, well, well, who'd've thought it?"

I found myself in the most spacious bedroom I had ever had the use of, with a small open fire which I discovered I could bank up and keep in for the evening by putting a thick layer of coal dust on top and then pouring water over the whole thing. My knowledge of science being minimal, I was unaware that I was slowly giving myself carbon monoxide poisoning until one of my drinking companions noticed that the silver ring I always wore had gone completely black. He urgently put me wise to the risks of my stoking activities.

I was also lent an electric kettle, which would mean the joy of a hot-water bottle at night, for the possibility of ever getting a hot bath with a 1930s boiler system and wartime coal rationing was, virtually speaking, nil. I reckoned I could wire up the plug without help, but when I studied the colours of the flex, they seemed not to correspond to any colour schemes I was acquainted with. Nothing daunted, however, I carried on, then filled the kettle, plugged it into the socket in the skirting board, and switched it on, only to be thrown backwards by the ensuing explosion. I picked myself up sheepishly and started fumbling around the blacked-out room for my torch. The first thing was to establish that no one had heard the bang, shatteringly loud though it had seemed to me. Luckily it was well after midnight. I opened my door cautiously and poked my head out into the corridor. A reassuring silence greeted me; in fact, an encouraging snore was coming from the neighbouring bedroom. The next thing was of course to mend the fuse so that I could see what damage I had done to the kettle. Spare fuse wire was something no self-respecting WAAF was ever without, if I could remember where I had put it. Having found it, I had to locate the fuse boxes. I vaguely remembered seeing something that answered to that description high up on the corridor wall outside my room. I sneaked out and started a tour of inspection. I was right. The beam of my little torch lit up an imposing row of boxes, so I carried a chair out into the corridor, climbed onto it, and, my torch between my teeth, started work.

I opened the door of the first box, pulled out the white enamel fuse plug, and replaced the blackened fuse wire with a new bit. I did the same with the second box, and with the third, only mildly surprised that my unfortunate miswiring had fused so many different circuits, but hoped that I would have enough new wire to finish the job. To my relief, boxes four and five seemed in good nick, but boxes six and seven needed attention, and by this time I was dribbling and my torch beam was beginning to waver.

But I made it to the end, and as I pushed in the last fuse plug, the corridor lights blazed on. I hurriedly got down, switched them off, and retreated into my now brilliantly lit bedroom, for to my surprise a bedside lamp that had never functioned had come on as well. With only a small bit of new fuse wire left for any fresh emergency, I decided to forget the kettle until daylight, even if it meant doing without a hot-water bottle. The excitement of the electrical chase had warmed me up, and I fell asleep at once.

When I lined up for my breakfast next morning, I heard one of the medical officers behind me in the queue saying something about a light that had never before worked in his room having woken him up by coming on in the middle of the night.

"Funny you should say that," said his companion, "Same thing happened to me!"

"What was that you said?" chipped in the senior Code and Cypher WAAF, whose snoring had reassured me during my repair work of the previous night, "I woke up in a blaze of unaccustomed light this morning! I'd often wondered why I couldn't get that bedside lamp to function. Most extraordinary! Wonder whatever it was?" I took my cup of tea and plate of rehydrated scrambled egg on soggy toast to a discreet distance from the speakers before risking a morning greeting to anyone else.

On the Admin side, apart from dealing with the paperwork of an increasing number of discharges, even if they were not complicated ones involving pregnant WAAFs, a genuine effort was being made to give them some preparation for life in the "real" world outside the service. Many of them had joined up on leaving school, or as soon after as they were allowed to, to become MT Drivers or Balloon Operators or Fitters, and in many cases they had had little further contact with family life, even if their original homes had not been bombed or their parents killed in raids. They may have complained bitterly about Air Force food, but they had never gone hungry.

Now they would suddenly have to cope not only with "home making"—if they could find somewhere to live—but with all the complexities of rationing and possibly with hunting for a job as well, to help pay for it all.

Two of the peacetime married quarters were therefore made over into centres for courses in various, mainly feminine, skills, and a WAAF Sergeant Cook was put in charge, with guidelines from Air Ministry in pamphlet form, as to what the courses should cover.

Sergeant [Dorothy] Bond, chosen to run this experiment, was in fact a very unusual woman. She was of country stock, had been in domestic service all her life until joining up, and could still call on her childhood's country lore to humanise the drabber aspects of "Make Do and Mend," and to bring a touch of humour to enliven the dullness of some of the boring but nourishing official recipes.

She was a large, "grenadier-type" figure, her long plait of mouse-coloured hair somehow wound round her head to accommodate her shiny-peaked WAAF cap, her stalwart legs in their thick grey lisle issue stockings and black, boatlike service shoes contributing to her heavy tread. She was not "Cordon-bleu," but that was to everyone's advantage. She offered instead tuition in "good, plain, English cooking," including what to do with a ration book, and had a healthy contempt for things in tins. She was also a good knitter, a traditional embroiderer, and a straightforward dressmaker, capable of taking an old garment apart and turning it into a new one.

The two houses were divided into cooking and catering in one, and what might have been called home care and dressmaking in the other. WAAFs who had applied for discharge were seconded from their other duties for whole days, or even did a week or longer with Sergeant Bond. I used to cycle round from time to time—Cranwell was a large site with two separate camps, East and West—to see how she was getting on and check on any problems or needs.

I think it was in September that the big Battle of Britain Parade was to be a march past Buckingham Palace. I can't remember how many WAAF from Cranwell were detailed to take part in this event, nor how they were selected. I think ultimately WAAF from all over the country were grouped together into a huge WAAF contingent. Some kind of a dress rehearsal was scheduled to take place at an airfield near London. The Parade was to be a March Past Buckingham Palace itself, where the King and Queen were to take the salute.

I had the good luck to be offered a flight to the assembly airfield, Haughton, in a small dual-control training aircraft. There were two spare seats behind me and the pilot, and Irene cadged a lift because she had a couple of days leave to stay with friends in that part of the country.

She didn't know what she was letting herself in for. Just before the war I had joined the National Women's Air Reserve, but too late actually to get into the air, though I had done some of the preliminary training. When I dropped a heavy hint to the pilot about this, he said cheerfully, "Want to take the controls?"

"Can I really?" I asked, with excitement.

"Sure. Carry on."

I had a marvellous time, ignoring the occasional gasp of horror from the seat behind me. When I saw what looked like our destination taking shape in front of us, I glanced questioningly at the pilot.

"OK. Circle the airfield for landing," he said, as though it were the most routine thing in the world. That was when I really thought Irene was going to have a heart attack, but the pilot took over before it was actually a question of making the descent.

The March Past was rather impressive, and we all had to do a sustained "Eyes . . . *right!*" without tripping over anything as we passed the specially built dais on which the royal couple were standing. I was fascinated to see the glorious Technicolour makeup which they had been subjected to. Even though colour photography was not yet in general use, makeup was probably still thought necessary to get the best results on the black-and-white newsreels of the time.

From VJ day onwards, RAF Cranwell's strength was gradually reduced. The Codes and Cyphers and other Technical Officers went first, the more mundane professions and skills, such as the Medical, Dental, and Equipment personnel being needed to ensure that those being discharged had all the proper checks beforehand and left with all the right equipment and papers. Needless to say we Admin types were the very last to leave.

Meanwhile, the mixed members of our Mess settled down to a very friendly existence, punctuated at intervals by farewell parties for departing drinking companions.

As the weather got colder, a gang of us—a couple of Medical Officers, one of the Dentals, and Irene and me—would get up logging parties and go off to a bit of untamed wood at the edge of the camp. There we would collect and saw up any bits of fallen trees to supplement the coal ration in the Mess grates. On returning we would cajole some dripping out of the kitchen staff and make dripping toast by the fire in the less-used anteroom still supposedly for WAAF if they should want to get away from the men.

One minor excitement about then was the posting to us of the first woman Padre, Elsie Chamberlain. I can't remember her rank, possibly Flight Officer. There were of course awful jokes before her arrival. Would she wear a male dog collar, or a bitch collar? If not, would she wear her WAAF collar and tie back to front? But not being a churchgoer, except under duress, I met her only in the Mess, looking, I have to admit, perfectly normal.

Amongst the people I "propped up the bar with" in the Mess was the officer in charge of the Aircraft Apprentices, of whom there was quite a big detachment on the station. He had come to the show I put on, and I had told him about the group of youngsters that I had produced plays with before the war.

"Do the apprentices ever do any drama?" I asked. "You wouldn't like me to do something with them, would you?"

He looked at me rather dubiously. "They're a bit of a rough lot," he said.

"Well, try me," I said, "if you think there'd be any takers."

So notices went up about a preliminary meeting to see what the response would be. I meanwhile more or less decided that Oliver Goldsmith's *She Stoops to Conquer* would be a good play to put on with them. A good number of them turned up at the meeting, and there seemed quite a lot of interest. So the next week we had an audition and a partial reading. I didn't want to intimidate any really bad readers amongst them, so I cast them mostly by hunch.

Their Education Officer was much intrigued by which ones had presented themselves. "You've got some conscientious lads there," he said, glancing through the list. "I see you've cast [John] Brunskill for Kate Hardcastle. Bright lad, that. Expelled from Harrow. You may have a bit of bother with him about keeping himself clean. Come back to me, if so. He'll either end up as Prime Minister or behind bars."

They were all between the ages of fifteen and seventeen, with one eighteen-year-old. They really enjoyed it, and those that didn't want to have parts painted all the scenery and helped with the lights.

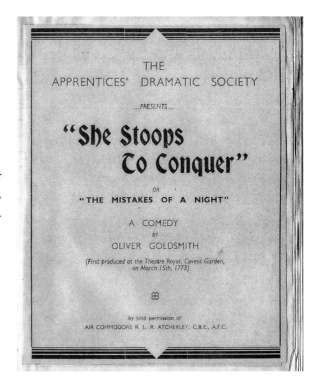

35. Program cover for
She Stoops to Conquer,
April 1945.

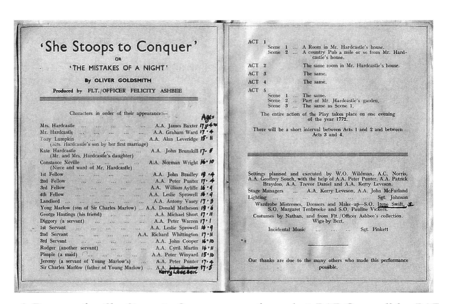

36. Program for *She Stoops to Conquer,* as performed at RAF Cranwell by RAF apprentices, April 1945. Note ages of actors.

37. *She Stoops to Conquer,* as performed at RAF Cranwell, April 1945. AA John Brunskill as Kate Hardcastle (left) with AA Donald Matheson as Young Marlow. "Young Marlow: 'But on coming closer to *some* women they don't look so old . . .'"

Brunskill made a most attractive Kate, and there was hilarious excitement about how to make bosoms for him and the other "ladies." I produced some WAAF bras, and the boys themselves found ways of filling them, including little balls of silver paper for nipples. They had great fun chasing the titties round the back of the stage trying to pinch them.

Their CO was much relieved that I didn't seem to need any protection. Perhaps it was partly the red flag still flying with the Union Jack on my bicycle that helped. The signatures on my programme are rather revealing. They range from "See you at Hyde Park Corner some time" and "Hope to see you leading the Reds parade after the Jubilee" to Brunskill's brief "Partners in Crime!" I was made an "honorary apprentice" after the last of the three performances, which took place just before Christmas.

38. *She Stoops to Conquer,* as performed at RAF Cranwell, April 1945. "Mr. Hardcastle (A.A. Graham Ward): 'A glass of wine sir if you please! . . . What! will none of you move?' Diggory (servant) (AA Peter Warren, *left*): 'I'm not to leave this place!'"

Station Commander at that time was Richard Atcherley, a Group Captain, commonly known as "Batchy," of Schneider Trophy Air Race fame. He was one of the identical Atcherley twins, tall, wiry figures, active and amusing. His twin, David, visited the base from time to time and was invited for Christmas of 1945.[2] The night before there was a lively party in the Mess, and when people came to breakfast the next morning, a number were seen clutching their hangover heads in disbelief at the sight of *two* Batchys side by side, tucking into their baked beans on toast.

2. The twin brothers David and Richard "Batchy" Atcherley gained a reputation as practical jokers. Richard then won world renown as a member of the RAF High Speed Flight in the Schneider Trophy Air Races of 1929.

There was a family event that Christmas, too. My sister Helen's Italian artist partner, who had been marooned in America during the war, had managed to get back to Europe. She, wishing to follow him, got round the complications about custody of six-year-old Tanya by pleading her widowed and aged (though not so ailing) mother as an excuse to get permission to take the child out of the country.

They arrived in Southampton a week before Christmas, and my mother and sister Mary went down to London to meet the boat train at Waterloo. There followed an interminable journey, with several changes at still darkened and unnamed stations, during which Helen's luggage, a cabin trunk with most of their possessions, got lost, only to be retrieved some weeks later with some of the most treasured things missing.

But at least they were able to celebrate Christmas together and only afterwards start debating how Helen would survive for the immediate future before possibly going to Italy or Paris. She had left Britain on marriage in 1938, as a musician, but had come back as a textile designer, and Manchester, the old Northern centre of the "rag trade," seemed an ideal jumping-off point as it was no great distance from Hest Bank, where my mother was living. And Helen was lucky. A successful and imaginative Jewish refugee from Berlin, Julius Frank, had advertised for another experienced designer for his studio, and Helen answered the ad. He fell for her at once, as well as for the designs she showed him, and offered her what at the time were fantastically favourable terms: £10 a week to work at home as and when she liked. This suited her very well because of Tanya, though her employer, of course, got her entire output.

She moved to Manchester, into the attic room of a gloomy board-and-lodging establishment in one of the city's grimier areas, and Tanya went to the local church primary school with a label tied round her neck in case she got lost. After a week there she pronounced, "The kids here are much *kinder* than my kids in New York." This Manchester connection turned out to be useful to me too, later on.

———•———

In the spring of 1946, the Charity Commission announced that it would not be staying in Morecambe. This meant that though Ted had still not been demobbed, Mary and the three children would eventually be moving from Hest Bank. Their return to London would leave my mother, now rising sixty-nine and becoming very arthritic, completely alone, about which we were all concerned.

And then I had an idea. By now the winding-down process at Cranwell was proceeding apace, and even Sergeant Bond's activities in the retraining of WAAF for civilian life were easing off and her own possible discharge date was drawing nearer. I cycled round to see her one day, and over a cup of tea asked her if she had any plans.

"Well, Ma'am," she said. "I've always had a dream to have a little boarding house of my own, but I don't think I could do that straight away. I'll probably go back into private service, for a bit anyway."

"I was wondering," I said, "if that's the way you were thinking. I believe you've always 'done for a gentleman'?"

"Yes, that's right, Ma'am. I've always been very lucky with my gentlemen."

"I suppose . . ." I hesitated over which words to choose, "You wouldn't at all consider 'doing for a lady' instead, would you?"

There was a pause. "I might." she answered, and smiled.

So I gave her a rundown on my mother, her unusualness, her sense of humour, her past life and interests, her current situation, and the fact that though not a stickler for protocol, she did still like to "have things nice."

"If you think it might be a possibility," I said, "give it a bit of thought. I'll be round again next week, and if you were interested, we could do something about arranging a meeting."

And that was the start of a seventeen-year "association" between my mother and Dorothy Bond. They met at the White Hart in Lancaster and got on like a house on fire. There was an almost feudal attitude to certain things in both of them that made the partnership work, helped by the greater classlessness of the north. We even came to think of her sometimes as "fifth daughter." Ex-Sergeant Bond moved in with my mother on the same day that Mary and the children left for London.

By that time my discharge date was on the horizon. But what *was* I going to do with myself? I had never given my future any thought at all. If I had, it would have been to assume that I would not survive the war.

What was I good for? I had a long-ago, rather uselessly fine-arts-based training, but nearly seven years of, what? in terms of employment.

And then I got an SOS from Helen in Manchester.

She had inspired her boss with the idea of a small team of art workers to hand-paint short runs of silk scarves (she had worked on something similar in New York) but now didn't want to take the responsibility of organising it herself!

"You'd be the perfect person," she said when I phoned. "It combines art training and administration. Super! Can't you come up and see him? Now! You can stay with me, here." So still in my uniform, I found myself sitting on the edge of a hard chair in Mr. Frank's little office. Helen's word was apparently enough for him.

39. 2213 Flight Officer Ashbee, J. F., RAF Cranwell, 1946.

"How much do you want to be paid?" he asked.

I didn't dare say £10 a week because that would look like collusion. "7 or 8?" I suggested.

"I'll give you £8," he said. "When can you start?"[3]

So on 25 July 1946 my time in the WAAF ended. I still have my buttons, very smooth from much polishing. My gratuity for nearly seven years of service was £16. I bought a wireless set with it, then already called a radio, one of those chunky-looking, liver-coloured, Bakelite jobs. At a party a year later in the flat I shared, it was knocked off the shelf and fell apart!

3. Felicity took the job as soon as she mustered out.

Felicity Ashbee: a chronology

Appendixes

Bibliography and Suggested Readings

40. Felicity Ashbee, woodcut. 1940. An illustration in the second number of the short-lived *WAAF* magazine "issued" by her and ACW Pyddoke at HQC during the first winter of the war.

Felicity Ashbee

A CHRONOLOGY

1913	22 Feb. Born at the Norman Chapel, Broad Campden, Chipping Campden, Gloucestershire, UK, second of four daughters of the architect and designer Charles Robert Ashbee and his wife, Janet (neé Forbes). Ashbee had moved his Guild of Handicraft from the East End of London to Chipping Campden in 1902.
1919	Moved with family to Jerusalem, where her father was an urban planner for British Mandate Palestine; attended American Colony School (See *Child in Jerusalem*).
1923–24	Moved to Forbes family home, Godden Green, Sevenoaks, Kent. Attended Mme. Honoré Kippington's Day School in Sevenoaks, Kent; then Miss de Ville's "Dame School."
1925–28	Attended Crofton Grange School, a boarding school, near Orpington, Kent.
1930	Sent to Hamburg, Germany, for a year to round out her education.
1931	At the end of her year of studies, her father flew her back to London's Croydon Aerodrome. This began her interest in flight.
1932–36	Attended Byam Shaw School of Art in Kensington, London, where she trained as a painter.
1936	First trip to Russia
1937–38	Designed Spanish Civil War posters. Joined Communist Party.
1938	Her painting *The Boatmen* hung in the Royal Academy Summer show.
1939	3 Sept. British Prime Minister Neville Chamberlain declared war on Germany.

14 Sept. Enlisted in Women's Auxiliary Air Force (WAAF). Stationed at Bentley Priory, near Stanmore, Middlesex, as Filter Room (radar) teller.

1940   Produced the first of her many shows, *Filtered Fragments,* to entertain the troops, which she did until she left the WAAF (see appendix B).

1941   Transferred to Intelligence and posted to Station X, Bletchley Park, Buckinghamshire.

29 June. Discharged as Corporal. Commissioned as Sections Officer. Posted to Loughborough, Leicestershire for one-month Administration Course.

1942   23 May. Her father, C. R. Ashbee, died.

Aug. Transferred to RAF Middle Wallop Fighter Bomber Station, Broughton, Hampshire. Assigned supervision of WAAF.

1943   Posted to Windermere in the Lake District for a one-month refresher course.

Posted to RAF Newbold Revel, Warwickshire.

Posted to RAF Ottercops Moss, Northumberland, a remote rural Chain Home radar post northwest of Newcastle near Hadrian's Wall.

1944   Posted to RAF Stenigot, near Donington on Bain, Lincolnshire. Promoted to Flight Officer.

1945   February. Posted to RAF Cranwell, Sleaford.

8 May. VE Day.

17 Aug. VJ Day.

1946   25 July. Discharged from WAAF. Given £16 gratuity pay.

With the help of her sister Helen, secured a job with a Manchester textile firm where she organized a small team of art workers to hand-paint short runs of silk scarves.

Worked as freelance artist, designing textiles.

1947   Moved to no. 71 Strand on the Green, London, sharing a flat with Mary Murphy.

1948   Part-time teacher of art at Staveley Road County Secondary Modern Boys' School, Chiswick.

1949	19 Sept. Part-time teacher of art for one year at Balmoral Road Secondary Modern School.
1950	April. Enrolled in Cooper's Hill Government Emergency Training College. Forced to withdraw in December after an accident to her knee during compulsory physical training. The school offered to let her begin again but she could not afford to continue training.
	Moved to 292 Edgware Road, London. Specialized in drawings of children.
	Began annual summer holiday travels (until 1998) to the Continent, including Italy, Spain, Greece, Yugoslavia, Turkey, North Africa, France, Poland, and Norway.
1951	11 May. Accepted post as visiting arts and crafts mistress at Crofton Grange School for Girls, Hertfordshire. A testimonial letter in December 1957 stated that she had taught there for six and a half years. She had attended this school as a girl. The school had moved from Kent in 1968.
1952	Illustrated Betty MacDonald's *Nancy and Plum* (London: Hammond & Hammond).
1954	London Council School evening instructor of painting and drawing.
1959	Began teaching art three days a week at Queen's Gate School, London. Served on editorial committee of *The Lot*, Queen's Gate yearbook.
1959–61	Taught part-time for Paddington Recreational Institute: Teddy Boys' Club 1959–60; First Feathers Club 1960–61; Moberly School for one month 23 Jan to 13 Feb 1961. Sent letter saying that "It's not worth the effort."
1961	8 May. Her mother, Janet Ashbee, died.
1962	Nov. Bought a house at 21 Courtnell Street, London, where she resided for the rest of her life.
1964	Made first of nearly twenty further trips to Russia, many to visit her cousin Ata in Moscow. Also visited Leningrad and her late great uncle George Carrick's sanitorium Janetovka in Ohrenburg, eastern Russia.

Began submitting short stories and essays for publication in periodicals. Eventually published nearly fifty.

Illustrated Guy H. and Claude A. Walmisley's *Tit-Willow or Notes and Jottings on Gilbert and Sullivan*. Privately printed, Farnham Common, Bucks: Beacon Press.

1967   Translated from the Russian Boris Balter's *Goodbye, Boys* (New York: Dutton). This was one of several of her Russian translations.

1970–2002   Made eight trips to United States following in her father's footsteps across the country, often lecturing about life in Chipping Campden.

1972   Published historic study "Balconettes: A Forgotten Aspect of Cast Iron," *The Connoisseur* (March). She had photographed and illustrated twenty-six examples found in London.

1978   Published "William Carrick: A Scots Photographer in St. Petersburg," *History of Photography* 2 (July 1978), 20–22. Inherited Carrick's collection of *cartes de visite*. Her mother's great uncle, Carrick was one of Russia's pioneer photographers. She lectured on the subject.

1979   July. Retired from teaching at Queen's Gate School.

1987   Published, with Julie Lawson, *William Carrick 1827–1878*. Scottish Masters Series 3. Edinburgh: National Galleries of Scotland.

1988   Lecture tour in Australia.

1998   Last trip to Moscow.

2002   22 Feb. Published *Janet Ashbee: Love, Marriage, and the Arts and Crafts Movement*.

2008   22 February. Published *Child in Jerusalem*.

26 July. Died at St. Mary's Paddington Hospital, London.

17 Sept. Interred in the Forbes-Ashbee family grave, Seal Parish Church near Sevenoaks, Kent.

2 October. Thanksgiving event to celebrate her life, held at the Art Workers Guild, Queen Square, London.

2009   26 April. *Felicity Ashbee: A Life of Her Own,* an exhibition to
        honor her life, Court Barn Museum, Chipping Campden,
        Gloucestershire.

APPENDIX A

Other Poems and Song Parodies Written During World War II

Other Poems Written During the War

Evacuees

What have you to complain of
    Oh foolish children of men?
You have changed the dirt of London
    For the green of the country again.
We shall have to put up with something
    Since the tide of war has caught us,
So why do you long for Leicester Square,
    When you can have "Two Waters"?
No longer on dusty pavements
    Do you have to push your prams,
You can hear the song of the thrushes
    Instead of the noise of trams.
Your child sees the front in the hedges,
    And is glad each day when he wakes;
Oh where is the lure of Peckham High
    When you can have "Hare-breaks"?

You will soon get used to the quiet
    Instead of the rush of cars,
And forget the Neon lighting
    As you learn the names of the stars.
The meadows will show their secrets,
    O foolish ones! Why do you yearn

For the sordid glamour of Oxford Street,
    When you can have "Sparrow's Herne"?

                                        (c. 1940)

Paris Has Fallen

A hawk hangs poised above the sunlit fields,
The uncut grass is vivid with June rain,
Children with gas-masks chatter off to school,
Paris has fallen.

Goose-stepping down the wide Champs Élysées,
Their heavy boots beneath Napoleon's arch,
Their rifle-butts put out the sacred flame;
Paris, Paris, Paris.

Machine-guns in the Place de la Concorde,
Heinkels above the towers of Notre Dame,
Paris has fallen.

"Tea in the garden, James, and strawberry jam,
These two people, I forget the name
Are dropping in—"
Paris has fallen.

"Stop-me-and-buy one" with its tinkling bell
Rings through the evening lanes, but lanes near Tours
Are packed with fear. A thousand hurrying feet
Push on, with mattresses, and prams piled high,
While close behind, the "iron castles" roll,
Mowing their passage through the meadow-sweet.
"We kept them out for seventy years; but now
We had no guns! Where were the '75s'?
We fought and fought, and died"—"Oh yes, and James,
Remind me to turn on the news at six."
The drone of Junkers over Fontainbleau,
Paris has fallen.

                                        (14 June 1940)

I Did Not Think

I did not think that I should ever know
Such utter emptiness since you are gone,
Or that it meant that I should miss you so,
And in a busy world be so alone.

There was so little time in which to share
The pleasures, and the sorrows, and the fears;
I put my hand out, and you are not there,
And once again I know the prick of tears.

I want you when the mist is on the hills,
I want you when the sun first floods the sky,
I want you in the coming dusk, that stills
The day-winds; then the small new moon climbs high.

How could we know, Fate would be so unkind,
As to take you, and leave me here behind?

                                        (1 September 1940)

The feel of dew-wet grass beneath bare feet,
Plums, just too ripe, that come clean from the stone,
A single raider's double-thudding drone,
The sound of sandals flopping down the street.
The warm, sweet smell of cows, the soothing touch
Of a soft sponge. The steady, gentle drip
Of water from the spring-board's matted tip.
We shared these things, and many another such,
These friendly, ordinary things we knew and loved so much.

White searchlights fingering the shifting cloud,
A brown back, that the sun's still hot upon,
The enchanting folly of a cheap French song,
Or in the dark, a poem said half-aloud.
All these delights were yours and mine to share,
Words were not needed between you and me;
But when forgetting it, I turn to see

Your answering glance—and find you are not there,
The stubborn tears trickle unheeded back into my hair.

(15 September 1940)

The tunnel is not very long, dear heart,
It has no bend,
And you can see the end,
Though fears beset you in the darkest part.
The light you hold,
A shadowy gleam of gold,
That is my love, and with you from the start.
Though the soft darkness as you first go through
Thrills you with fear,
And close beside your ear,
Strange whisperings and doubts beleaguer you;
Brush them away!
You will soon reach the day,
Where I await you, and my love still true.

(October 1940)

I would not have you weep
Heart of my heart,
Sleep.
My hands are yours to hold,
My heart to keep.
Tho' dark unholy things
Seek to enfold
You, with thick shuttered wings,
And round you crowd,
Whisper my name aloud,
And I am near.
No loneliness nor fear
Can break the magic thing
Which we two hold.
Thro' the wind's blustering
My heart to yours shall sing,
Proud!

(10 October 1940)

Bletchley Park

> It takes all sorts to make a park
> But we must admit we're rather in the dark,
> To set our minds at ease
> Will somebody tell us please,
> What Bletchley's ever done to get such queer evacuees,
> Still it takes all sorts to make a park.

In the back-streets of Bayswater there exists a demimonde
Of girls, whose life is just one awful bore,
But since Officers are fond
Of almost anything that's blonde,
Bayswater's moved to Bletchley for the war.

> It takes all sorts to make a Park,
> But we must say we're completely in the dark,
> Whether they are really able
> To *buy* coats of mink and sable,
> And why they try to talk like June and look like Betty Grable,
> Still it takes all sorts to make a park.

In Cambridge, grave professors dominate each College Hall
A Brains Trust, so to speak, whose word is law,
But at England's stirring call
To her sons both great and small,
The Brains Trust moved to Bletchley for the war.

> Well it takes all sorts to make a Park,
> And their bite is much less fearsome than their bark,
> It must be such an awful strain
> To have a really brilliant brain,
> And to find, when one is middle-aged the brilliance starts to wane,
> Still it takes all sorts to make a Park.

The students of St Hilda's, Hugh's and Lady Margaret Hall
Are the flower of English girlhood, rich and poor,
What mere man could fail to fall
For these sirens, lithe and tall
Who are beautifying Bletchley for the war?

> It takes all sorts to make a Park,
> But, in passing, we would make just one remark:
> However dowdy they may look

Their souls the sour of Rupert Brooke
And St. Francis of Assisi—oh, if only they could cook!
But it takes all sorts to make a Park.
The gentlemen of Bloomsbury are artistically inclined
Any sudden sort of noises they abhor
High explosive bombs, they find
Disturb their peace of mind
So Bloomsbury moved to Bletchley for the war.

It takes all sorts to make a Park
Still we must admit we're rather in the dark
What perverted kind of joy
Can it give to annoy
The world at large by wearing suits of gaudy corduroy.
Still it takes all sorts to make a Park.
Angular mem-sahibs mixed with aged maiden aunts
In the peacetime Bournemouth lounges they adore,
But one dare not take the chance
Of living quite so close to France,
So Bournemouth moved to Bletchley for the war.

It takes all sorts to make a Park,
But their style of dress went out with Noah's Ark,
They will undoubtedly endorse
The view that we are rather coarse
But those strange projecting teeth remind us strongly of a
horse.
Still it takes all sorts to make a Park.
Yes it takes all sorts to make a Park
Tho' we feel the future outlook's rather stark.
When we watch the crowds that pour
Past the sentry at the door
We're not so sure that England's going to win the ruddy war.
Still it takes all sorts to make Park.

(c. 1941, Bletchley Park)

The shallow river, lapping lazily
A drowsy passage thro' the quiet land
Lingers; until the banks close narrowly

And rocky walls constrain on either hand.
Then, gathering energy,
    Foaming, he meets the sea.

2.

Strong is the wind that can no outlet find,
Wilder his pow'r, the narrower his way;
The Flame is fiercer when it is confined,
More white the heat of its intensity.
So the bewildered heart seeks boundary.

3.

Blustering wind, the sheltered flame that sears,
River in purpose bright;
So will the heart, when it no longer fears,
In bondage light,
Stride singing thro; the gateway of the years.

(10 November 1943)

The Poem

Grey-green beech-trunks lit by the fading sun,
Stretching bare-finger'd winter tracery,
Their earth-bound roots sunk in October's gold.
The sudden flight of a Spitfire from its lair
In careless pride, lifting and spiralling.
From hidden huts, a plume of static smoke,
The whirr of a pigeon's wing in the quiet air;
Stillness that needs no words. A breathing-space
Of timeless peace, snatched from a warring world.

(7 November 1943)

The Song

Smooth grey beeches lifting to the sky
The fingers of their winter tracery;
The sudden flight of a Spitfire from its lair
In careless pride, curving and spiralling;
The beat of a pigeon's wing thro' empty air;

Stillness that needs no words. An interval
Of quiet peace, snatched from a warring world.

(8 November 1943)

I do not care if morning never comes,
Nor the grey fields appear,
Pale solace are the twinkling Pleaides,
Jewelled Orion, Cassiopeia's chair,
And all the glory of the winter skies
When the dark trees obscure.
Wakeful I lie, and thro' the thrumming air
The triumph of man's intellect goes forth
To kill and be destroyed.
And over Europe's arc of belching flame
Castor and Pollux dwindle in the glare;
Pegasus rears his nostrils at the stench
Of acrid cordite, and of burning flesh;
Is this man's aim?
How shall the bloody earth yield fruit afresh,
The charred and smouldering stones be built again?
Then thro' the tangled branches of the trees, my eyes encounter
Watching above the clamour of the fight,
Serene and hopeful still, the constant Plough,
Tilling the quiet furrows of the night.

(December 1943)

The darkness presses on the window-pane,
Draw tight the curtains, make the fire glow,
Shut out the things I do not want to know,
Quiet; and just the needles of the rain.

And in that quiet, stranger thoughts are freed,
To knock and clamour at the waiting heart,
Seeking the whole, in which to be a part;
For to be wanted is a human need,

My mind is there to use, my hands to take,
They wait to labour for the common good;

What talents I possess are meant to share.
I want to give! And giving, I could make.

Perhaps tho', in the encircling solitude
The future steals upon me, unaware.

(December 1943)

"The beachhead is expanding!
As our armour pushes forward . . . (thro' the fig-trees and the vines)
Tanks and stores and guns continue landing . . ."
Commandos pick their way thro' hidden mines,
Trampling the little paths from secret beaches.
Petrol fumes . . . not pines.
"Our forward troops have captured two small islands . . ."
Where once, a boat chugged out into the bay,
With grapes from Lavendou, and cheese, and wines,
And bold Explorers!
Who found, that magic day,
By sunbaked paths too hot for sandalled feet
A Sleeping Beauty's Castle, strange and still,
All overgrown with tamarisk and thorn;
And daring us to pass,
An empty snakeskin stretched across the way!
How long before the clamour dies: How long
Till red-winged crickets in the brittle grass
Fill the warm quiet with their reedy song?
Will this year's wine be sweet?

(17 August 1944)

Under the sky I stand,
Watching the scarlet tractor in the corn,
The golden corn
That bends and shimmers on the curving land
Ruffled by passing winds.
The evening light seeps from the quiet sky,
And suddenly, I do not understand . . .
Why am I so afraid?
My little span in the vast arc of time,

This friendly block of years I call my own,
What is it worth?
A drop of water on a world of stone.
It's not as tho' I were afraid to die;
For when the candle-flame of life goes out
What is there left to fear?
Just, that this troubled, warm, and friendly earth
Is known to me . . . and dear.
The corn is sheaved, the purring tractor gone,
High in the dark a hidden plane sets forth,
And on the fretwork of the wireless masts
The warning lights go on.

(August 1944)

Song Parodies Not in the Present Volume

You Are My Corporal
(To the tune of "You Are My Sunshine")

I joined the Air Force to serve my country
In the only way I knew,
And indirectly, I'm killing Nazis
With my curried rice and stew.

You are my Corporal, my only Corporal,
You are my boy in Air Force Blue,
I peel potatoes, I mash up carrots,
In a fever of love for you.

Though my beef-olives are rather blackened
They're stuffed with kisses through and through,
When my potatoes burst from their jackets,
They are bursting with love of you.

There's so much love in my treacle-puddings,
It give them quite a purple hue,
But when I see yours go in the swill-bin,
It nearly breaks my heart in two.

You are my Corporal, my blue-eyed Corporal,
Smile at me from the breakfast-queue,

And if my nose is a little shiny,
It's reflecting my love for you.

Closing Chorus for *Shuddering Heights*
"We wish you luck as you wave us good-bye"

Sung by the cast only:

That's the story of Shuddering Heights,
And we've come to the end of our play
Draw the curtains and turn out the lights,
For it's time that we went on our way.
Give us a cheer, for we've liked coming here
May we come again one day?
Wish us luck as you wave us good-bye
Cheerio as we go on our way.

Sung by the entire cast of the show who have come onto the stage:

Wish us luck as you wave us good-bye,
Cheerio as we go on our way.
Wish us luck as you wave us good-bye,
With a cheer, not a tear, make it gay.
Give us a smile we can keep all the while
In our hearts while we are away,
Wish us luck as you wave us good-bye,
Cheerio, as we go on our way.[1]

---

1. "Wish Me Luck" is a very well known wartime song sung by the very popular former English music hall comedienne Gracie Fields, to RAF troops during the war. To hear the song, see websites for Gracie Fields.

Show Log Book

Felicity wrote and directed most of the sketches and songs for her shows. She used some over and over again, often modified to reflect the situations and moods of military life at the time of the performance. Each of her shows consisted of short comedy sketches (skits), dances, music, songs, and song parodies—except for the last, which was a production of Oliver Goldsmith's play *She Stoops to Conquer.*

41. Show log book. Record of shows with the WAAF produced by J. F. Ashbee S/O. 1941–1945.

The program summaries given below are taken from Felicity's self-bound scrapbook, which contains printed programs, tipped-in letters, photographs, and many inscribed notes.

I. *FILTERED FRAGMENTS.* Bentley Priory, June 1941.

    1. Opening Chorus

    2. Waltz Ensemble

    3. Raw Bodies, a sketch (see Appendix C)

    4. Solo Tap Dance

    5. Violin Solos
       Piano Solos

    6. Missing Government Property, a sketch

    7. Harmony Quartet

    8. Solo Ballet Dance

    9. Songs: "Trees" and "So Deep Is the Night" (sung by Felicity)

    10. Violin Solo
        Piano Solo

    11. The WAAF Officer's Selection Board, a sketch (see Appendix C)

    12. Tap Ensemble

    13. Closing Chorus

II. *BLUE AND KHAKI NO. 2.* The Army, Navy, and Air Force Revue. RAF Station X, Bletchley Park, 19–20 December 1941.

Part I

    1. Opening Chorus

    2. Christmas Crackers, Dancing Troupe

    3. Raw Bodies, a sketch

    4. Songs: "Passing By" and "Yeomen of England"

    5. "The Dying Duck," a dance, being the 57th farewell performance of Madame Orlova (who danced at the Imperial Court of Russia in 1901), inadequately supported by Sacha Flopoff, on the piano.

    6. Look Before You Listen, a sketch

Part II

A Privy Council, a sketch

Part III

    1. Post No. 99, a song

    2. Dangerous Age, a sketch

    3. Songs: "Two Shanties"

    4. Night Club Special, a sketch with dancers, cornet, and guitarists

    5. Board with Darts, a sketch

    6. Closing Chorus

III. *BLUE AND KHAKI NO. 3*. Station Wing, 24 April; RAF Station Leighton Buzzard, 25 April; 2 at RAF Station X, Bletchley Park, 29–30 May 1942.

Part I

1. Opening Chorus by the WAAF, Corps of Military Police, and the Pioneer Corps
2. Dance, WAAF dancing troupe
3. Tap Dance
4. The Woman's Place, a sketch
   Part 1. A.D. 1242
   Part 2. A.D. 1942
5. Crooner: "I Know Why" and "Apple Blossom Time"
6. Monologue: The Way to Accept Him
7. Songs: "Fishermen of England" and "I Walk Beside You"
8. The Bowl of Rice, a sketch
9. Unspoken Words, a sketch

Part II

1. Dance and Singer
2. Flossie at the Granada, a sketch
3. Crooner: "When I Love, I Love" and "The White Cliffs of Dover"
4. Uniform Thoughts on the Park, a poem
5. Songs: "The Cobbler's Song" and "Russian Serenade" (in Russian)
6. Tap Dance
7. Corporal Otis Regrets and My Sister and I, parodies
8. Shuddering Heights, A tragic and gripping Victorian melodrama in four scenes.
9. Finale

IV. *ANGELS OVER BASE*. RAF Middle Wallop, December 1942.

Hullo Middle Wallop!
Hullo Middle Wallop!
This is "D" Watch Calling!
This is "D" Watch Calling!
We now Present: ANGELS OVER BASE
Are you receiving us? Over.

1. Opening Chorus
2. Tap Dance

3. Flossie at the Granada, a sketch

4. My Sister and I, sketch

5. Solo Tap Dance

6. WAAF Officer's Selection Board, a sketch (see Appendix C)

7. The Shadow Passes, a sketch

8. Corporal Otis Regrets, a parody

9. Time Marches On, a sketch

10. Tap dance solo

11. Nightmare Ballet

12. Closing Chorus

V. *OUT OF THE SUN.* Middle Wallop, 22 February 1943.

1. Opening Chorus

2. Double Tap number

3. Raw Bodies, a sketch

4. Harmony Trio

5. Women at War, a sketch

6. Acrobatic Dance

7. Health and Beauty, a sketch

8. You Are My Corporal, song parody

9. The Bowl of Rice, a ghost story

10. Cook's Septet

11. Skipping Tap Dance

12. I'm Dreaming of a White Nighty, song parody after Irving Berlin's White Christmas."

13. Barcarole, dance and duet

14. Shuddering Heights, a melodrama

15. Closing Chorus

VI. *THE STARS LOOK DOWN.* RAF Middle Wallop, 25 May; RAF Ibsley, 30 May 1943. Assisted by the Station Band.

On 28 May 1943, 3 items of the Show were revived for a concert for *Wings for Victory* at the Guildhall, Andover.

1. Opening Chorus

2. Kit Inspections, a sketch

3. Victorian Ballads

4. Dance

5. Parsons of Puddle, a sketch

6. Songs

7. International, a sketch

8. Opera parody (The Guardians of Seville) [see Appendix C]

9. Banjo

10. Guardroom 53BC Caveman Style, a sketch

11. My Promotion, song parody of "My Devotion"[1]

12. The Mysteries of Udolpho, a play[2]

VII. *THE SHOW GOES ON!* RAF Andover, 25 October; RAF Middle Wallop, 26 October 1943.

Assisted by the Station Band

1. Opening Number

2. The Woman's Place, a sketch

3. Piano Solo

4. Dance

5. Brain Trust, a sketch

6. Duets

7. Occupied Territory, a sketch

8. Inside Story, a sketch

9. Musical Clothing Parade, song parodies

10. Crime Club (also called The Killer Gang), a sketch

11. Conjuring, a sketch

12. Mock Circus with acrobats and a "horse"

13. Closing Chorus

VIII. *NEW AND BOLD.* RAF Church Lawford, 19 January; RAF Newbold Revel, 21 January 1944.

1. Opening Chorus

2. The Woman's Place. A sketch

3. Turn

4. Kit Inspections, in Germany and the South Seas, a sketch

5. Songs

1. Popular song by Roc Hillman and Johnny Napton (1942).

2. Written in 1793 by Ann Radcliffe; a burlesque radio version given by BBC and adapted for this show. Permission was granted by the author, Margaret Nelson Jackson, to use her burlesque with adaptations by Ashbee for use on the stage.

6. The Bowl of Rice, a sketch

7. Recorder solo

8. Brain's Trust, a sketch

9. Crooning

10. Turn

11. Shuddering Heights, a play

12. Closing Chorus

IX. *WAKEY-WAKEY.* RAF Stenigot, 19–20 November; RAF Market Stainton, 24 November 1944.

1. Opening Chorus

2. Songs

3. Crime Marches On: A Women's Auxiliary Luftwaffe, a sketch

4. Song

5. Dance

6. Anna (a Russian/Tolstoy parody)

7. Songs

8. Killer Gang, a sketch

9. Song: "I Never Slept a Wink Last Night"

10. Mess Meeting, a sketch

11. Ventriloquist

12. Piano Solo

13. Opera Parody

14. Closing Chorus

X. *THE SHOW GOES ON (AGAIN!).* RAF Cranwell, 24 and 25 April; RAF Swinderby, 26 April 1945.

1. Opening

2. Crime Marches On, a sketch

3. You Are My Corporal, song parody

4. Flossie at the Granada, a sketch

5. Songs: "Shine Thro' My Dreams," "Smiling Thro'," "Lover Come Back to Me"

6. Killer Gang, a sketch

7. Dancing Time

8. 3 o'clock in the Morning? ? ?, a sketch

9. Lease-Lend, a sketch

10. I'm Dreaming of a White Nighty, song parody of Irving Berlin

11. Shuddering Heights, a melodrama

XI. *SHE STOOPS TO CONQUER* or "The Mistakes of the Night" (Play by Oliver Goldsmith, 1773) (RAF Cranwell, 16, 17, and 18 April 1945).

Cast composed entirely of Aircraft Apprentices between the ages of 15 and 18. All women's parts played by boys who also painted scenery, managed stage, curtain, lights. Costumes from Nathan's and from Ashbee's collection. Five instrumentalists from RAF College Orchestra provided incidental music.

APPENDIX C

Three Drama Sketches

Felicity wrote "Raw Bodies" and "WAAF Officer's Selection Board" in 1941, for her first show, *Filtered Fragments*. She mounted the initial performances at Bentley Priory on 12 June 1941, less than a year after she had joined the WAAF. She revised "Raw Bodies" for future performances in December 1941 and in February 1943, developing the plot and including more stage directions. This is the original text. She drew the characters, especially that of Duncan, from her own experiences in "WAAF Officer's Selection Board."

Skit One: "Raw Bodies"

"A" Watch (Filter)

Characters

    A Drill Corporal (ex-vaudeville star)

    9 WAAF recruits

(Recruits standing sloppily and aimlessly; they look scruffy and uncertain. Enter Cpl., briskly.)

CPL: So, we're all here, and ready for drill. I believe you have all done some before you came here?

(The recruits nod emphatically.)

    Then you will remember that the first and most important point is to obey *all* commands *implicitly*, regardless of how they may appear to you. (recruits nod again) Right. Falling in on a marker (pointing in the smallest); you can be Marker. Marker, *fall IN!* (Marker looks wildly round, finally stumbles forward a couple of paces).

CPL: *Squad, on your marker FALL IN!*

(All nine recruits plunge frantically onto the marker and fell her to the ground.)

CPL: (ironically) You seem to have forgotten your instructions a little, you should be on the *Left* of, not *ON* the marker (she pulls them about). Now then, *Right*

Dress! (All clutch the skirt of the recruit on their right. Cpl. groans.) No, NO! (reciting) On the command *Right Dress,* the whole with the exception of the 3rd right-hand woman heads to the right! Now then, *Right Dress!* (They do it.) That's better. Squad will advance, *Right Turn.*

(Some recruits turn to the right, some step forward, some hesitate and turn to the left. In the confusion one recruit loses one of her shoes. After order has been restored . . .)

CPL: You don't seem very sure of that; once more pirouetting the *right* heel and left toe. Squad *one!* (scooting motion begins) Squad *two!* (all try and stead themselves on each other) A little better . . . I think we'll leave that and turn to saluting. Saluting to the *front* by numbers (all, prematurely, start trying to salute their bosoms). No, *no,* you, Marker, come out and try it. On the command squad bring the right leg up in a circular movement towards the head. That's right, higher . . . higher . . . (props her up, the others gape). No, no, I'm forgetting (giggles) we're the other side of the footlights now, aren't we? Once more, no, the right *arm.* Thumb and forefinger straight. *So* (forces recruit's arm into the right position). Now . . . A new A.M.O. has just been issued with instructions that all ranks shall salute *two or more aircraft* when passing over-head. We'll just run through that. The command is given: *Squad, on top salute!* *1, 2, 3, 4, 5,* (bends over backwards saluting the sky). Is clear?

(A good deal of confusion ensues, falling over backwards, etc. The airwoman cursed with "dead men's shoes" loses both shoes in what now amounts to a rug-ger scrum. The Cpl. pulls her out.)

CPL: What's the matter with your shoes? Speak up!

RECRUIT: (looking round wildly) They're "dead men's shoes" (she is holding them in either hand).

CPL: (seizing them) Oh, you mean second-hand ones (recruit nods). Wouldn't the Sergeant at Equipment give you any others? (recruit shakes her head) H'm. Look a bit big. Well, we can't stop for that now. You must keep them on as best you can (offers her own garters). Right, now. *Squad number!* (a good deal of muddle and business). You must practice that on your own. While you're queuing up for meals is a good time. We will now take a rather more advanced movement only used on State Occasions. *Squad. Attention!* The success of this maneuver depends entirely on the speed and accuracy with which it is carried out. *Undress by numbers.*

(Recruits remain impassive, the full meaning of her words not having penetrated. They are not very quick in the uptake.)

CPL: Squad by numbers *Undress!* 1, 2, 3, 4, 5, (Still uncomprehending the recruits obey as instructed and start unbuttoning tunics and skirts; suddenly a voice is heard off[stage], calling: "Cpl. Cpl. You're not busy, come here a moment, will you?")

(CPL. exits with an arabesque.)

The recruits stop one by one and look at each other. Slowly as it dawns upon them that they are well-embarked on something approaching a strip tease act, they cover their mouths with their hands, stifling horrified squeals, and clutching their trailing garments, [they] scatter in all directions.

CURTAIN

* * * * * *

Skit Two: "WAAF Officer's Selection Board"

A sketch

"A" Watch (Filter)

Properties:

1 long table, 5 straight-backed chairs, pen tray, pencils, notepaper, upright calendar, ashtray

Characters:

    G/Officer Personby-Personby

    W/Officer Hamilton-Burke

    S/Officer Prendergast

    Miss Pinkerton (Miss Batts)

    Applicants: Duncan, Darley, and Dibbs

G/OFF: We have quite a number of applications before us today, for Admin. C. and Filter Duties, (I'm not altogether sure what the latter entails, but we'll discuss that later). Right. Just touch the bell Prendergast, will you.

PREN: Certainly, Ma'am.

G/OFF: Sit down. Your name is Duncan. I see you were at Bedford High School (significant looks) and think that you took a degree in higher mathematics.

DUNC: Yes, Ma'am.

G/OFF: You like maths?

DUNC: Yes, Ma'am.

G/Off: You do . . . I see. You seem to have travelled quite extensively; we should like to know a little about that.

Dunc: Yes, Ma'am. I have travelled in Italy, Germany, and Russia; I also took a group of children out to the Fairbridge Farm School in Australia.

G/Off: Do you mean to infer that these were working class children?

Dunc: Oh, yes, Ma'am, the Fairbridge scheme is essentially for workers' children.

G/Off: I see . . . Hmm . . . (more glances) . . . You say that you have been to Russia. I hope that does not imply that you have been interested in the views held by that unfortunate country.

Dunc: I felt that it was a great experiment, Ma'am.

G/Off: You did. Hmm, I see apart from that that you were a buyer . . . is it? at Bourne and Hollingsworth.

Dunc: Yes, Ma'am . . . a very interesting job.

G/Off: But hardly a very suitable one for a prospective officer.

Dunc: It was a job entailing a good deal of responsibility Ma'am.

G/Off: I am fully aware of that . . . You have a hobby?

Dunc: I am very interested in languages, Ma'am.

G/Off: Yes, quite. Would you like to ask some questions Hamilton-Burke?

H.B.: Yes. I see you come from Fighter Command. How long were you there?

Dunc: A year, Ma'am.

W/Off: You were happy in your work?

Dunc: Yes, Ma'am.

W/Off: Have you any comments to make on the hostel, the food, and so on?

Dunc: Well, Ma'am, we usually slept in a room intended for four, and queued up for three-fourths of an hour for a slice of bread and marge, but apart from that and the fact that we only had one bath a month, I have no complaints.

W/Off: One bath a month is all that regulations permit of, and should be quite sufficient for the rank and file.

G/Off: Quite sufficient. Have you any questions, Prendergast?

S/Off: Yes, Ma'am. Were you a prefect at school?

Dunc: No, Ma'am.

S/Off: Have you done any Girl Guide work or Women's Institute work?

Dunc: No, Ma'am.

S/Off: No prison work even.

Dunc: No, Ma'am.

S/Off: Do you play badminton?

Dunc: No, Ma'am.

S/Off: It is taken for granted that you have no political interests or connection.

Dunc: Nothing exceptional, Ma'am.

S/Off: No foreign relations or course.

Dunc: Only one Russian cousin three times removed, a refugee in Venezuela.

S/Off: I see. That's all, Ma'am.

G/Off: Miss Pinkerton, would you like to ask a question?

Miss P: Now tell me you may be perfectly frank. Do you take sugar or salt on your porridge?

Dunc: Well I . . . er . . . to be perfectly candid I don't ever eat porridge.

G/Off: Well Duncan I think that is all. Oh just one more thing. Do you drink?

Dunc: No, Ma'am. I am a teetotaler.

G/Off: Right. You may go.

(exit Duncan)

W/Off: Very little to recommend the girl, I'm afraid, what do you feel Personby—Personby?

S/Off: Well to start with she's not been to Roedean,[1] secondly all this foreign stuff seems highly undesirable, she plays no badminton, and if that were not enough she doesn't drink and would be perfectly useless for social activities in the mess. No there seems to be no question about it. She is not the type we want. You agree, Miss Pinkerton?

Miss P: Quite.

G/Off: We'll take the next one. Touch the bell Prendergast.

(enter Darley)

G/Off: Sit down. Your name is Darley. You appear to [have] been at a comparatively unheard of establishment for Gentlemen's Daughters, followed by a finishing school in Paris. Is that right?

Darley: That's right, Ma'am. A perfectly topping hole, we had a marvelous time.

(Ma'ams wince)

G/Off: You were a debutante in 1939 and presented? Correct?

Darley: Right again, Ma'am. Ostrich feathers and all that. Wizard!

G/Off: And . . . er . . . do I understand that you have done some work as an artist's model?

Darley: Must find something to fill the old purse with, Ma'am . . . can't scrounge all the time . . . try to keep off the streets . . . you know.

---

1. Prestigious independent girl's school founded in Brighton over 125 years ago.

G/Off: Quite, quite. Any questions, Hamilton-Burke?

W/Off: You come from Fighter Command? What was the hostel like and the food and so on?

Darley: Oh SUPER Ma'am. Each had a separate room with H & C laid on, and always a savoury after the sweet.

W/Off: And baths?

Darley: Boiling hot water all the time, two baths a day if we wanted them. Troops can't be too clean you know to make up for other deficiencies.

G/Off. That will do. Over to you, Prendergast.

S/Off: You realize that you will probably have NO cypher work to do. Are you prepared to do a considerable amount of administrative duties?

Darley: Suits me, Ma'am—nothing to it really.

S/Off: You may be on a station where there is *no* female companionship.

Darley: Couldn't be improved upon, Ma'am.

S/Off: Have you any past-time such as embroidery for instance?

Darley: Oh, YES, Ma'am. I use to work till one in the morning doing cross-stitch when I was in civve-street.

G/Off: Right. Prendergast? Miss Pinkerton?

Miss P: Just one little matter. Which do you prefer *people* or *things?*

Darley: Oh, ANimals.

G/Off: Oh, one point, Darley. Do you play golf?

Darley: My handicap is 6, Ma'am.

G/Off: That will do Darley. You may go.

(exit Darley)

G/Off: Not a particularly nice type of girl, and not really the officer type; I don't know I'm sure, but . . .

W/Off: Some of her remarks struck me as being definitely peculiar and her manner not very reassuring . . . but . . .

S/Off: She has not been to Roedean . . . but . . .

G/Off: That of course is the gravest drawback, but in the circumstances and seeing that her golf handicap is 6 . . . (quite remarkable in one so young), I think that we can feel quite satisfied in passing her. (others agree) Now we come to this question of the Filter Commission . . .

W/Off: Have you any idea what it really entails?

S/Off: I wondered. Filter. Filter. Could it have anything to do with swill? Rather technical, y'know . . .

G/Off: I think not, Prendergast. I have heard that it has something to do with tiddlywinks . . . tho' I fail to see the necessity to make it a commissioned rank.

W/Off: I am quite of the same opinion, however our hands are tied. We have our instructions in the matter. We'll have to pass her.

S/Off: I have grave doubts about these technical commissions. However, let us continue.

(S/Off touches bell)

G/Off: Sit down. Your name is Dibbs. I gather you have had some education, (aside: educated at home) and that you are only 18. What kind of work have you been doing?

Dibbs: I was a Fighter at Plotter Command.

S/Off: You mean a Flighter at Potter Command . . .

G/Off: No. No. No, the girl was a Plotter H.Q.F.C.

W/Off: You realize you will probably have to work 24 hours a day 7 days a week with very low pay no promotion and no leave.

G/Off: No leave of course.

Dibbs: Yes, Ma'am.

W/Off: You will probably not be working with very congenial companions.

Dibbs: No, Ma'am.

G/Off: Not under very desirable conditions.

Dibbs: No, Ma'am.

W/Off: Little air and no opportunity for sports or exercises.

Dibbs: Yes, Ma'am. I mean no, Ma'am.

S/Off: You may even be living under canvas.

Dibbs: Yes, Ma'am.

G/Off: You still wish to take the commission

Dibbs: Oh, yes, Ma'am.

G/Off: Miss Pinkerton . . . Miss Pinkerton.

Miss P: Now tell me, could you give an injection to a dog with hysteria?

Dibbs: I could . . . but it depends on the size of the animal.

G/Off: That will do, you may go.

(exit Dibbs)

G/Off: Well, there are no comments. The girl must be passed in any case . . . unless Miss Pinkerton has any views.

Miss P: Yes I have. Firstly my name is not Pinkerton but BATTS . . . Miss Batts. Secondly, the girl cannot possibly be certified.

G/OFF: Certified. Certified? What do you mean?

MISS P: Well what are we on a Lunacy Board for if not to certify.

G/OFF: Lunacy Board, Lunacy Board . . . This is an Air Ministry WAAF Officer's Selection Board . . . and . . .

MISS P: My God, what day is it. This is Friday the 13th isn't it? It's not? Well I'm on the wrong Board then. I must fly. I'll be seeing you.

W/OFF: Scandalous!

G/OFF: Preposterous!!

S/OFF: Incredible!!

(general consternation ensues, during which the telephone rings. G/Off lifts up the receiver)

G/OFF: Hullo! Hullo! Who is that? (aside to W/Off) Preposterous behavior . . . these civilians . . . no proper sense of duty . . . Hullo, yes! G/Off Personby-Personby . . . yes, speaking. Oh is that the Colonel? (giggles) . . . um! You silly one. No! yes . . . um. NO, I'm not busy (aside to S/Off) Defer the other applicants till tomorrow. Yes, of *course* dear . . . I'm free now! All right . . . 12 then . . . at the Regent Palace!!

CURTAIN

* * * * *

Skit Three: "The Guardians of Seville"

A Mock Opera

A story of Greed and Passion, and of the final triumph of Virtue.

The piece was performed in *The Stars Look Down* for RAF Middle Wallop, 25 May; and RAF Ibsley, 30 May 1943. Assisted by the Station Band.

The scene is laid in the Boudoir of Donna Eemobily, who is seen as the curtains open reclining on a couch: she sings

> One fine day he'll marry me
> And in his arms he'll carry me;
> I am delighted
> For our troth is plighted
> United we will ever be!
> When the clock strikes half past three.
> Oh! Don Riggormortis!

42. Felicity's costume sketch for Don Riggormortis.

You will come to visit me,
Oh! Don Riggormortis![2]

DONNA E. (rec.)[3]: Alack, the time is long in coming! My niece and ward Amouretta, she it is conspiring to frustrate me. Till I possess her rubies, which are large, and of quite exceptional quality, my lover Don Riggormortis cannot afford to wed me!

AMOURETTA (rec.): Good-day my aunt and my guardian! I hope you have had an enjoyable siesta.

2. From Act 2 of Puccini's *Madama Butterfly* ("Un bel di vedremo").

3. The recitatives (rec.) were improvised. Thanks to Patrick Murphy for information about this skit.

DONNA E. (rec.): Yes thank you, Amouretta. (Aside) The sight of those jewels puts me in a torment. (To Amouretta.) What are you waiting for?

AMOURETTA (rec.): Dear Aunt, I come to beg you for a trifle. Could you oblige me a little money? My pins and hair ribbons are very scruffy and I must purchase new ones in the market.

DONNA E. (rec.): Oh Grasping Amouretta. Will you never have enough?

("Duet" from Humperdinck's *Hansel and Gretel*)

DONNA E.: I have nursed you from a child,

  Saved you from the tempests wild,

  Silk and satins bought you,

  All my learning taught you,

  To my bosom pressed you,

  With my love caressed you,

  This unkind behaviour

  To your Aunt, your Saviour,

  Makes me hate to see your face

  And wish you in a hotter place.

AMOURETTA: Cruel Aunt, you are unkind;

  Nothing's further from my mind

  Than the thoughts you mention;

  I am all attention.

  See, my tears are flowing

  Anguish I am knowing,

  My suspense is growing,

  You look very angry.

  Oh! Dear Aunt, don't vent your fury on me!

(Exit Donna E. in stately rage leaving Amouretta in tears.)

AMOURETTA (rec.): What fearful purpose is she now intent on?

  Unhappy Amouretta!

  How desperate is your lot!

(She weeps. Enter Pepeeto through the window)

PEPEETO (rec. aside): Ah! What is happening? My loved one, and in tears! Amouretta!

AMOURETTA (rec.): Pepeeto! Ah, how glad I am to see you.

  But be careful, this is not the place for you.

PEPEETO (rec.): Nor for you, either. I come to take you from your cruel guardian.

Aria: From *Holy City*)[4]
> Elope with me, elope with me.
> Come, let us steal away
> Together, dear Amouretta,
> We'll greet another day.

AMOURETTA (rec.): Ah, sweet Pepeeto, how I long to follow;
> but if I do, my jewels I relinquish.

PEPEETO (Aria)
> Elope with me, elope with me,
> Hark to my plaintive cry.
> Compared with my adoration
> What things can jewels buy?
> Beloved Amouretta!
> I'll love you till I die.

(Donna E.'s voice is heard off, calling, "Amouretta").

PEPEETO (rec.): Heavens. We are surprised.

(He gets under the bed).

(Enter Donna Eemobily, holding a paper).

DONNA E. (rec.): Idle again! Now I have had enough!
> You are unworthy of the love I've lavished on you.
> I am incensed! I'll brook no more excuses.

PEPEETO:
(rec. putting head from under bed):
> Unhappy situation. What will she do now?

AMOURETTA (rec.): My dearest Aunt.
> See how I kneel before you, to ask your forgiveness.

DONNA E. (rec.): No, not a word. My patience is exhausted!
> No more forgiveness,
> No more forgiveness shall you get from me!

(Exit Donna E., dragging the protesting and weeping Amouretta behind her.
(Pepeeto emerges from under the bed.)

---

4. A Victorian parlor ballad (1892) with music by Michael Maybrick (writing as Stephen Adams) and lyrics by Frederic Weatherly.

PEPEETO:

(Aria. "Soldier's Chorus," from Gounod's *Faust*)

    What are these terrible things I hear?

    Poor little Amouretta dear!

    This is no moment to shed a tear.

    Now I must think out a plan . . . to escape.

(Sounds of approaching singing are heard).

DON RIGGORMORTIS:

(Aria, heard offstage)

    Toreador, oh tum ti tum ti tum!

    Toreador, Toreador!

    In through the window to my little turtle dove,

    Where are you hiding, my love?

    Don Riggormortis waits below,

    Toreador,

    Let me my passion show!

(rec.) My plans are all completed, and by careful craft and guile, I soon shall have
    my ward and nephew's fortune safe in my keeping.

PEPEETO (rec.): What further tales of horror are unfolding?

    Oh, wicked uncle!

DON R. (rec.): I only need his signature and all will then be mine.

    Oh, Donna Eemobily

(Enter Donna E. They embrace).

(Duet: *Il Baccio*)[5]

BOTH: Ah, how I adore you

    And implore you

    To embrace me, Dear Heart;

    How I miss you,

    Till I kiss you,

    But now I've good news to impart.

DONNA E. (solo): I have plans now afoot

    To bring us the loot

    And then far away we will fly!

DON R. (solo): I too have it taped,

---

5. From Luigi Arditi's waltz-song "Il Bacio" (the kiss).

Not much has escaped

My eye.

Ha! Ha! Ha! (etc. to end of verse).

(Pepeeto emerges from under bed, and sings, aside)

PEPEETO (rec.): This is too much. I can stand it no longer

(Aria: "Anvil Chorus" from Verdi's *Il Trovatore*

Now with righteous scorn Pepeeto's heart is bursting,

And in anger for a just revenge he's thirsting.

Bursting! Thirsting!

Scheming! Screaming!

(At end of aria Pepeeto plunges two daggers simultaneously into the backs of Don Riggormortis and Donna Eemobily.)

PEPEETO (rec.): So that will pay you double dealing villains.

(Don R. and Donna E. stagger and fall to the ground, in stages as they begin to sing):

Duet: (From Saint Saens's *Samson and Delilah*)

DON R. AND DONNA E.: Ah! It is fulfilled! And I am killed,

It's no good crying,

Death is on the wing, I feel his sting,

For I am dying.

Ah! here I implore thee, see here I implore thee,

Ah! once again then say you adore me!

(repeat as desired)

(They die finally, and Amouretta rushes in. She flings herself into Pepeeto's arms)

AMOURETTA (rec.): Ah! Pepeeto! My Saviour! From what dread future have you

rescued me? Your grateful Amouretta now embraces you.

Duet: Pepeeto and Amouretta ("La Donna e mobile" from Verdi's *Rigoletto*)

Donna Eemobily, finished ignobily,

Dead as a tortoise, is Riggormortis

No longer fearful

Frightened or tearful,

We can be cheerful,

They are both dead!

Ah . . .

They are both dead!

(these final lines are sung with Pepeeto and Amouretta embracing, each with a foot on one of the corpses.)

FINIS

Bibliography and Suggested Readings

Ashbee, Felicity. *Child in Jerusalem.* Syracuse: Syracuse Univ. Press, 2009. With an introduction by H. G. F. Winstone.

———. *Janet Ashbee: Love, Marriage, and the Arts and Crafts Movement.* Syracuse: Syracuse Univ. Press, 2002. With an introduction by Alan Crawford.

———. "William Carrick: A Scots Photographer in St. Petersburg." *History of Photography* 3 (July 1998), 209–22.

Crawford, Alan. *C. R. Ashbee: Architect, Designer, and Romantic Socialist.* Yale Univ. Press, 1985.

Escott, Beryl E. *The WAAF.* Oxford: Shire Books, 2007.

Gough, Jack. *Watching the Skies.* London: HMSO, 1993.

Korda, Michael. *With Wings Like Eagles: A History of the Battle of Britain.* New York: Harper Collins, 2009.

Lysons, Daniel, and Samuel Lysons. *Counties of England.* 6 vols. (1806–1822).

McCarthy, Fiona. *A Simple Life: C. R. Ashbee in the Cotswolds.* Berkeley: Univ. of California Press, 1981. Reissued by Faber Finds in 2010.

Nobel Lectures, Physics 1912–1962. Amsterdam: Elsevier Publishing Co., 1964.

Reed, Cleota. *Felicity Ashbee: A List of Her Literary Work.* Syracuse: The Arts and Crafts Society of Central New York, 2009.

———, comp. and ed. *Felicity Ashbee, as We Knew Her.* Chapbook. Syracuse: The Arts and Crafts Society of Central New York, 2011.

Reed, John. *Ten Days That Shook the World.* 1919.

Salzman, L. F. *The Victoria History of the County of Warwick.* Vol. 6, 1951.

Walford, Edward. *Greater London: A Narrative of Its History, Its People, and Its Places.* 2 vols. London: Cassell, 1883–84.